Documents and Debates
The Chartists

DOCUMENTS AND DEBATES

The original titles in the series (still available):

Sixteenth Century England 1450–1600	Denys Cook
Sixteenth Century Europe	Katherine Leach
Seventeenth Century Britain	John Wroughton
Seventeenth Century Europe	Gary Martin Best
Eighteenth Century Europe	L.W. Cowie
Nineteenth Century Britain	Richard Brown and Christopher Daniels
British Social and Economic History 1800–1900	Neil Tonge and Michael Quincey
Nineteenth Century Europe	Stephen Brooks
Twentieth Century Europe	Richard Brown and Christopher Daniels
Twentieth Century Britain	Richard Brown and Christopher Daniels

For the extended series, see the back of this book.

Documents and Debates
General Editor: John Wroughton M.A., F.R.Hist.S.

The Chartists

Richard Brown

Houghton Regis Upper School, Bedfordshire

Christopher Daniels

Royal Latin School, Buckingham
Sometime Schoolmaster Fellow Commoner,
Sidney Sussex College,
Cambridge

MACMILLAN

First published 1984 by
THE MACMILLAN PRESS LTD
Houndmills, Basingstoke, Hampshire RG21 2XS
and London
Companies and representatives
throughout the world

ISBN 0–333–36249–7

A catalogue record for this book is available
from the British Library.

Printed in China

Reprinted 1986, 1987, 1991, 1993

To G. W. D. and B. D.

To Jayne and Dawn, who counted
and to Margaret, who made the coffee

Contents

General Editor's Preface

This book forms part of a series entitled *Documents and Debates*, which is aimed primarily at sixth formers. The earlier volumes in the series each covered approximately one century of history, using material both from original documents and from modern historians. The more recent volumes, however, are designed in response to the changing trends in history examinations at 18 plus, most of which now demand the study of documentary sources and the testing of historical skills. Each volume therefore concentrates on a particular topic within a narrower span of time. It consists of eight sections, each dealing with a major theme in depth, illustrated by extracts drawn from primary sources. The series intends partly to provide experience for those pupils who are required to answer questions on documentary material at A-level, and partly to provide pupils of all abilities with a digestible and interesting collection of source material, which will extend the normal textbook approach.

This book is designed essentially for the pupil's own personal use. The author's introduction will put the period as a whole into perspective, highlighting the central issues, main controversies, available source material and recent developments. Although it is clearly not our intention to replace the traditional textbook, each section will carry its own brief introduction, which will set the documents into context. A wide variety of source material has been used in order to give the pupils the maximum amount of experience – letters, speeches, newspapers, memoirs, diaries, official papers, Acts of Parliament, Minute Books, accounts, local documents, family papers, etc. The questions vary in difficulty, but aim throughout to compel the pupil to think in depth by the use of unfamiliar material. Historical knowledge and understanding will be tested, as well as basic comprehension. Pupils will also be encouraged by the questions to assess the reliability of evidence, to recognise bias and emotional prejudice, to reconcile conflicting accounts and to extract the essential from the irrelevant. Some questions, *marked with an asterisk*, require knowledge outside the immediate extract and are intended for further research or discussion, based on the pupil's general knowledge of the period. Finally, we hope that students using this material will learn something of the nature of historical inquiry and the role of the historian.

John Wroughton

Acknowledgements

The editors and publishers wish to thank the following who have kindly given permission for the use of copyright material:

Associated Book Publishers for statistics from *The Victorian Economy* by F. Crouzet, published by Methuen & Company; Basil Blackwell Ltd for extracts from *The Condition of the Working Class in England* by F. Engels; Cambridge University Press for tables from *The Abstract of British Historical Statistics* by B. R. Mitchell and P. Deane, and *British Economic Growth 1688–1959* by P. Deane and W. A. Cole; The Editor, Victoria History of the Counties of England (Institute of Historical Research) for an extract from *Victoria History of Hertfordshire*, Volume IV; Hodder & Stoughton Ltd for extracts from *The Industrial Revolution, 1750–1850* by R. M. Reeve; The Librarian, The Bodleian Library, for extracts from *Letters Relative to the Chartists 1839–40*; Oxford University Press for a chart from *British Economy of the Nineteenth Century* by W. W. Rostow.

Every effort has been made to trace all the copyright holders but if any have been inadvertently overlooked the publishers will be pleased to make the necessary arrangement at the first opportunity.

Chartism – an Introduction

In their *Bibliography of the Chartist Movement 1837–1976* J. F. C. Harrison and Dorothy Thompson say that

> Chartism is. . . a richly self-documented subject which has left behind an enormous number of printed documents, newspapers, journals, pamphlets, broadsides, hand-bills and posters. . . .

There is an embarrassing richness of evidence which historians can use whether they are operating on a national or a local level. Chartism is the best documented of all the radical movements of the first half of the nineteenth century. This is hardly surprising since it dominated much working-class radical activity for nearly twenty years. Chartism was an inescapable dimension of British society at *all* levels. It epitomised the hopes and fears of all contemporaries – a new society? a just society? a democratic society? a new Establishment? No wonder that people from Queen Victoria downwards commented upon it, pondered its implications and passed judgements about it. The emphasis which many Chartists placed upon literacy also helps to explain the plethora of evidence. Chartism was in part the response of a literate and sophisticated working class. Although not all Chartists could read, written and printed material was an important part of their lives and the emphasis placed upon education and literacy can clearly be seen in Lovett and Collins' *Chartism* published in 1840.

Chartism is probably the most difficult of all nineteenth-century radical movements about which to make generalisations. This is partially a result of the nature of the evidence available. Harrison and Thompson argue that

> despite the rationality and sophistication of much Chartist literature, the motivation behind the actual movement operated at a different level. Feelings of outrage and class hatred everywhere pervaded Chartism, and the tone was often more violent than was usually to be found in the published material. . . .

Also there is an inherent ambiguity in what a Chartist actually was. There were 'moral force' Chartists, 'physical force' Chartists,

Teetotal Chartists, Complete Suffrage Chartists, Municipal Chartists, Church Chartists – the list is almost endless. Only their acceptance of the Charter allows us to use the blanket term of 'Chartist' at all.

Why did the 1830s spawn so many different variants of a 'Chartist'? We know why Chartism developed. It was a response to the conditions created by changes in the economy and by the growth of towns *but* it was not just an urban phenomenon. There were rural Chartists. It was above all a demand for political rights which have their origins long before any industrial changes took place. Only a Parliament elected by Universal Suffrage would remove the social evils under which the labouring population suffered. It was both practical and utopian. Yet even the intensity of working-class condemnation of conditions did not create a unified movement. Chartists may have agreed about ends but certainly not about means. The Chartists of Bradford differed from those of Glasgow and from those of Ipswich and Gloucester. This fatal flaw was evident from the outset among both leaders and rank and file. It can be seen clearly in the Convention of 1839 and was still unresolved nine years later. Chartism was fatally weakened from within by the inability of its leaders to agree about just how the Charter was to be implemented. This was an expression of the cultural, economic and social diversity of Britain. Class relations had not replaced the older social relationships based upon deference and paternalism even in some of the industrial cities. It is doubtful if there was a working class as *one* social class in 1850, let alone 1830. In these circumstances unity was short-lived and almost invariably pragmatic. Ideological unity in itself was insufficient to achieve ideological change.

Power did not fall into the streets as it did in Russia in 1917. The 'authorities', either locally or nationally, never lost the initiative for any significant period of time. If they did for a while they generally sat back and allowed the Chartists to run out of steam. The 'authorities' knew how to use their power. The Chartists did not. They failed to use their greatest weapon to any real effect by not managing to convert mass support into mass power. Demonstrations, strikes, petitions, meetings, mobs all showed mass support but most Chartist leaders were unwilling to push this support in the direction of revolutionary or violent change. Despite what some of the aristocracy believed, Britain in the 1830s and 1840s was different from most European countries where radical change could not be accommodated within the existing social system. In Britain there were riots, effigies were burnt, property was attacked *but* for most people the existing social system, for all its defects, remained supportable and, in certain circumstances, modifiable. For all the rhetoric, diatribe, oratory and demagogy revolutionary change was the viewpoint of a very small minority even within Chartism.

So why was there mass support for the Charter and its aims? Chartists believed in a better society and saw the Charter and Universal Suffrage as their means of achieving this. By a 'better society' they meant one in which there was no 'distress' and in which they were treated fairly. Chartism was thus strongly influenced by economic conditions. The industrial crisis from 1836 to 1842 corresponded to the first two phases of Chartist activity. The third phase in 1848 was also marked by economic distress. Working people flocked to the Charter and became active – the Newport rising was in 1839, the Plug Plot in 1842, Kennington Common in 1848 – but even a slight economic improvement led to support dissipating in other directions. Some Chartists saw a 'better society' in a retrospective sense. Chartism was a means of returning to working conditions before technological change made them obsolete. This can be seen in the attitude of the handloom weavers and other outworkers and also in the naïve agrarian utopianism of O'Connor's Land Plan. Cheaper food prices from the mid 1840s, a result of changing techniques of production as much as the repeal of the Corn Law in 1846, and the acceptable face of capitalism obviated the psychological need for Chartism. The 1850s saw Chartism as an increasingly minority concern though the objectives contained in the Charter retained their focusing power. The Reform Act of 1867 was the triumph of the 'respectable' face of radicalism.

The eight chapters in this book cover the main events within Chartism. The opening chapter places Chartism in its context and through it you should be able to understand why Chartism occurred. The second and third chapters cover the objectives, methods and issues raised in the years between 1836 and 1840. What direction should Chartists take? This is followed up in the chapter on the leaders and rank and file which looks at the diversity of the movement and the reasons why Chartists could not agree. Chapters 5 and 6 cover two trends evident in 1842 – the economic distress which led to the Plug riots, and the attempt to achieve union between middle- and working-class radicals in the Complete Suffrage League. Both failed to achieve their initial promise as did the Chartist Land Plan considered in Chapter 7. The final chapter examines the events of 1848 when many contemporaries saw Chartist activity at its most dangerous. The fiasco of Kennington Common is a fiasco only with hindsight.

We have approached Chartism from both a chronological and a topical viewpoint. It is important that you have a clear idea of the chronology of Chartism and you will be asked to produce narratives from documents on several occasions. This should provide you with a clearer notion of the sequencing of events and allow you to make analytical judgements with more confidence. As Ranke wrote over a century ago, a historian needs a real affection for this human race in all its manifold variety. . . . If he feels this affection for the living being as such, he will enjoy seeing how man had perennially contrived to live . . . he will readily follow the development of his nature under such diverse conditions, his institutions and his morals, the sequence of events and the development of major enterprises – all this he will try to follow without any purpose beyond the pleasure in individual life itself.

I Dimensions of Change – a Scenario for Chartism

A historical sequence or a movement like Chartism is the product of many agents, each with their own sequence. As a result historical causation is rarely, if ever, logical. It is the historian who assesses importance, identifies trends and creates order from the rubbish heap that is primary evidence. As Fernand Braudel has said: 'History exists at different levels. . . . There are ten, a hundred levels to be examined; ten, a hundred different time spans.' This chapter looks at the changing fabric of British society in the early nineteenth century from four separate, though interconnected, viewpoints. Just what was the impact of industrial and especially technological change upon a society and workforce accustomed to traditional economic values? Not surprisingly, contemporaries disagreed about the precise effects of industrialisation. Some, like Thomas Carlyle, emphasised the debilitating impact of change on the labouring population. Others, like Ure and later Samuel Smiles, saw economic growth and increased productivity as beneficial. Did the 'standard of living' of the working population decline or improve? Can the historian objectively talk about 'good' and 'bad' effects of change?

The second section of the chapter allows you to examine the changes evident in contemporary statistics. Professor Court rightly counsels caution in their use since quantitative material, indisputable though it may be, can only become meaningful historically if translated into human terms. It is both the individual and people with whom the historian is truly concerned. But numbers can provide a partial explanation of historical events, especially if related to the succeeding sections on living and working conditions and the political dimension. Was Chartism a class movement? What do we mean by 'class' in this context anyway? You need to consider the genesis of 'class'. Can we talk about a working 'class' in 1830? or 1850? Is the term working 'class' meaningful in this period? How prevalent were the older, pre-industrial social values? These are some of the questions which you will need to examine while identifying the parameters within which Chartism developed and the issues to which it addressed itself.

We have identified only four dimensions of change but there were others which played a vital role. Religion? Culture? Occupation?

Geography? Consider as many as possible and then ask yourself just how far you have reached in the direction of what Braudel christened 'total history'. He may use the phrase to express an ideal but he is correct to believe that we should be trying to understand the multi-perspective nature of the past. Chartism was not caused by one or even five trends or causes, but emerged out of a social milieu in which a large proportion of the population perceived that there were social evils, economic inequalities and political injustice. Chartism was diverse in its origins and diverse in its character and chronology. Though as historians we all have specialisations, as different people we study different fragments of the past, we must *never* lose sight of the ultimate aim of fitting the pieces into a whole.

1 Impact of Industrial Change – Contemporary Reactions

(a) Were we required to characterise this age of ours by any single epithet, we should be tempted to call it, not an Heroical, Devotional, Philosophical, or Moral Age, but, above all others, the Mechanical Age. It is the Age of Machinery, in every outward and inward sense
5 of that word; the age which, with its whole undivided might, forwards, teaches and practises the great art of adapting means to ends. Nothing is now done directly, or by hand. . . . Our old modes of exertion are all discredited and thrown aside. On every hand, the living artisan is driven from his workshop, to make room for the
10 speedier, inanimate one. The shuttle drops from the fingers of the weaver, and falls into iron fingers that ply it faster. . . . What changes too, this addition of power is introducing into the Social System; how wealth has more and more increased, and at the same time gathered itself more and more into masses, strangely altering the old
15 relations, and increasing the distance between the rich and the poor. . . . Not the external and physical alone is now managed by machinery, but the internal and the spiritual also. Here too nothing follows its spontaneous course, nothing is left to be accomplished by old natural methods. Everything has its cunningly devised imple-
20 ments, its pre-established apparatus, it is not done by hand, but by machinery. . . .

Thomas Carlyle 'Signs of the Times' first published in 1829; printed in A. Shelston, *Thomas Carlyle – Selected Writings* (Penguin, 1971), pp 64–5

(b) The impressions of those days are very vivid; I can call their images, though they have been long in their coffins: I must see the grandchildren of those I saw when I first came to Manchester, for I see my own grandchildren and I see now men who are of my own
5 age, and even younger than me, but who have passed their lives in

mule-spinning. Their intellect has shrunk up and become dry like a tree, and they have become children again, and they are not the same men that I remember them to have been. I know many such instances.

> Evidence of Titus Rowbotham, aged 51, a worker from Macclesfield, given to the Factory Commissioners in 1833; printed in *Report of Factory Commissioners* 1833, examinations taken by Mr Cowell, p 48

(c) And all the Arts of Life they'd change into the Arts of Death in
   Albion:
   The hour-glass contemn'd because its simple workmanship
   Was like the workmanship of the plowman, & the water wheel
5 That raises water into cisterns, broken & burn'd with fire
   Because its workmanship was like the workmanship of the
      shepherd;
   And in their stead, intricate wheels invented, wheel without
      wheel,
10 To perplex youth in their outgoings & to bind to labours in
      Albion
   Of day & night the myriads of eternity: that they may grind
   And polish brass & iron hour after hour, laborious task,
   Kept ignorant of its use: that they might spend the days of
15   wisdom
   In sorrowful drudgery to obtain a scanty pittance of bread,
   In ignorance to view a small portion & thinks that All,
   And call it demonstration, blind to the simple rules of life.

> William Blake, 'Jerusalem'; printed in William Blake, *Poems and Prophecies* (Dent, 1972), pp 238–9

(d)   Look yonder where the engines toil:
          These England's arms of conquest are,
          The trophies of her bloodless war:
             Brave weapons these.
5,   Victorious over waves and soil,
          With these she sails, she weaves, she tills
          Pierces the everlasting hills,
             And spans the seas.
          William Thackery, 1852

(e) Gather, ye Nations, gather. From forge and mine and mill
   Come Science and Invention: Come, Industry and Skill
   Come with your woven wonders, the blossoms of the loom.
   That rival Nature's fairest flowers in all by their perfume.
5 Come with your brass and iron, your silver and your gold
   And arts that Change the face of earth, unknown to men of old.

Gather, ye Nations, gather. From ev'ry clime and soil,
The New Confederation, the Jubilee of toil.
Lyrics by Charles Mackay which were set to music by Henry
Russell to commemorate the Great Exhibition of 1851

(f) This island is pre-eminent among civilized nations for the
prodigious development of its factory wealth. . . . This very pre-
eminence, however, has been contemplated in a very different light
by many influential members of our own community, and has even
5 been denounced by them as the certain origin of innumerable evils to
the people and of revolutionary convulsions to the state. . . . I believe
such allegations and fears will prove to be groundless, and to proceed
more from the envy of one ancient and powerful order of the
commonwealth, towards another suddenly grown into political
10 importance than from the nature of things. . . .
Andrew Ure, *The Philosophy of Manufactures*, 1835, pp 6–9

Questions

a   What do these extracts tell you about the different contemporary
reactions to economic changes?
b   How far do you think does Thomas Carlyle demonstrate that the
early nineteenth century was 'the Age of Machinery'? What
impact does he maintain industrial change has had?
c   What evidence do Carlyle, Rowbotham and Blake provide to
show the debilitating effects of industrial change?
d   How do Thackery and Mackay evoke the benefits of change in
their poems?
e   How does Ure explain the misunderstandings that have occurred
about the effects of change? How valid do you find his assertion?
* f   'The economic gains brought about by the industrial revolution
took place at the expense of social conditions for the labouring
population.' Discuss.

2   The Statistics of Change

A figure, a table, or a graph can be critical in economic history, for it
may bring to the final test our view of how or why things happened.
At the same time it must be allowed that much statistical work is in
the nature of description rather than explanation. . . . Quantities may
assist to define the limits of a problem, even if they do not serve to
solve it.
W. H. B. Court in *Approaches to History*, H. Finberg (ed.),
1962, p 29

Table 1 Great Britain, population, 1801–61

	Population (millions)	Increase %
1801	10.49	—
1811	11.97	14.1
1821	14.09	17.7
1831	16.26	14.0
1841	18.53	12.3
1851	20.82	11.1
1861	23.13	12.7

Source: B. R. Mitchell and P. Deane, *The Abstract of British Historical Statistics* (Cambridge University Press, 1962), p 6

Table 2 Great Britain, population, birth, death and marriage rates 1811–61 (per thousand)

	Births	Deaths	Marriages	
1811–20	26.6	21.1	—	*(estimates)*
1831–40	36.6	23.4	—	*(estimates)*
1841–45	35.2	21.4	15.7	
1846–50	34.8	23.3	16.5	
1851–55	35.5	22.7	—	
1856–60	35.5	21.8	—	

Sources: Mitchell and Deane, op cit and N. L. Tranter, *Population since the Industrial Revolution* (1973), p 53

Table 3 England and Wales, population, composition of population by age groups, 1821–51 (by thousands and as a percentage of the total)

	1821	%	1841	%	1851	%
70+	311.3	2.95	446.9	2.81	503.3	2.81
60–9	480.7	4.56	699.4	4.40	808.8	4.51
50–9	694.4	6.59	1,026.2	6.45	1,253.1	6.88
40–9	983.3	9.30	1,526.6	9.64	1,767.6	9.00
30–9	1,243.2	11.9	2,051.5	12.9	2,364.7	13.2
20–9	1,657.3	15.7	2,833.4	17.8	3,137.1	17.5
10–9	2,218.2	21.1	3,318.9	20.8	3,670.6	20.5
0–9	2,942.7	27.9	4,011.2	25.2	4,440.4	24.7

Source: As for Table 2

Questions

a What is the major source of information used in calculating population after 1801? What difficulties does it pose for the historian?

b Why did the death rate rise in the 1830s and the late 1840s?

* c Why do historians not agree about why population changed in this period?

d Which was more important, the death rate or the birth rate, in the increase in the population of Great Britain after 1830?

Table 4 Industrial production, estimated output of coal industry 1800–50 (million tons)

1800	11.0	1835	27.7
1816	15.9	1840	33.7
1820	17.4	1845	45.9
1825	21.9	1850	49.4
1830	22.4		

Source: P. Deane and W. A. Cole, *British Economic Growth 1688–1959* (Cambridge University Press, 2nd edn, 1969), p 216

Table 5 Industrial production, net output of principal textile industries in Great Britain 1805–60 (£m)

	Cotton	Woollens	Linen	Silk	Total	National income %
1805	10.5	12.8	7.6	2.0	32.9	10
1821	17.5	16.6	12.5	3.0	49.6	14
1836	21.8	16.7	8.4	6.5	53.4	11
1845	24.3	21.1	8.4	6.5	60.3	11
1850	21.1	20.3	8.7	7.0	57.1	10
1855	26.2	20.2	9.0	8.0	63.4	10
1860	33:0	21.2	9.4	9.0	72.6	9

Source: Deane and Cole, op cit, p 212

Table 6 Industrial production, new versus old technology

	Powerlooms	Handloom-weavers
1795		75,000
1813	2,400	212,000
1820	14,150	240,000
1829	55,500	225,000
1833	100,000	213,000
1835	109,000	188,000
1845	225,000	60,000
1850	250,000	43,000
1861	400,000	7,000

Source: F Crouzet, *The Victorian Economy* (Methuen, 1981), p 199

Table 7 Industrial production, estimates of pig iron output in Britain 1796–1852 (thousand tons)

1796	125	1840	1,396
1806	244	1847	1,999
1823	455	1852	2,701
1830	677		

Source: R. M. Reeve, *The Industrial Revolution 1750–1850* (London, 1971), p 214

Questions

a   How can we use these statistics to produce a chronology of industrial growth between 1800 and 1850?
b   It is difficult to date the origins of industrial change. The point of take-off varies from industry to industry and even within industries. How do these tables demonstrate this?
c   Economic change often implies technological obsolescence. How could you use Table 6 to explain this?

With the development of industry the proletariat not only increases in number; it becomes concentrated in greatest masses, its strength grows, and it feels its strength more. . . . Machinery obliterates all distinctions of labour and nearly everywhere reduces wages to the same low level. . . .
> Karl Marx, *The Communist Manifesto*, first published 1848 (Penguin edn, 1967), p 89

Table 8   Prices: average prices of wheat 1800–50 (five-year averages: price per imperial quarter)

	s	d		s	d
1800	84	11	1830	63	0
1805	72	11	1835	48	6
1810	101	3	1840	64	7
1815	84	11	1845	55	3
1820	65	11	1850	42	10
1825	60	5			

Source: R. M. Reeve, op cit, p 232

Table 9   Wages: indices of average wages 1800–50 (1840=100)

1800	95	1831	101
1805	109	1840	100
1810	124	1845	95
1815	117	1850	100
1820	110		
1824	105		

Source: P. Deane and W. A. Cole, op cit, p 23

Table 10   Wages: a Bolton handloom weaver 1797–1830

	s		s	d
1797	30	1816	12	
1800	25	1820	9	
1805	25	1824	8	6
1810	19	1830	5	6

Source: G. R. Porter, *The Progress of the Nation*, 1847 edition, p 457

Table 11   *'Social tension' and its components*

	Trade cycle pattern	Wheat price (actual annual average: s. per quarter)	Wheat price (abstracted; inverse)	'Social tension'[1]
1790	3	50.5	3	6
1791	4	45.0	4	8
1792	5	41.2	5	10
1793	0	47.7	4	4
1794	1	51.8	3	4
1795	$2\frac{1}{2}$	74.1	$\frac{1}{2}$	3
1796	3	77.1	0	3
1797	0	52.8	4	4
1798	1	50.2	5	6
1799	3	67.6	2	5
1800	4	113.7	$\frac{1}{2}$	$4\frac{1}{2}$
1801	3	119.0	0	3
1802	5	67.2	4	9
1803	1	56.6	5	6
1804	$1\frac{1}{2}$	59.8	4	$5\frac{1}{2}$
1805	$2\frac{1}{2}$	87.5	2	$4\frac{1}{2}$
1806	3	79.0	3	6
1807	2	73.3	4	6
1808	1	78.9	3	4
1809	4	95.4	2	6
1810	5	106.1	1	6
1811	0	94.6	$1\frac{1}{2}$	$1\frac{1}{2}$
1812	1	125.2	0	1
1813	$1\frac{1}{2}$	108.5	1	$2\frac{1}{2}$
1814	$2\frac{1}{2}$	73.9	3	$5\frac{1}{2}$
1815	3	64.2	5	8
1816	0	75.6	3	3
1817	3	94.8	0	3
1818	5	84.2	$\frac{1}{2}$	$5\frac{1}{2}$
1819	0	73.0	1	1
1820	1	65.6	3	4
1821	$1\frac{1}{2}$	54.3	4	$5\frac{1}{2}$
1822	2	43.2	5	7
1823	3	51.9	3	6
1824	4	62.1	1	5
1825	5	66.7	0	5
1826	0	56.9	$\frac{1}{2}$	$\frac{1}{2}$
1827	$1\frac{1}{2}$	55.9	1	$2\frac{1}{2}$
1828	2	60.4	$\frac{1}{2}$	$2\frac{1}{2}$
1829	0	66.0	0	0

Table 11 *continued*

	Trade cycle pattern	Wheat price (actual annual average: s. per quarter)	Wheat price (abstracted; inverse)	'Social tension'[1]
1830	1½	64.4	0	1½
1831	2	66.3	0	2
1832	0	58.7	1	1
1833	1	53.0	3	4
1834	2	46.3	4	6
1835	3	39.4	5	8
1836	5	48.4	4	9
1837	0	55.6	3	3
1838	1	64.3	1	2
1839	3	70.6	0	3
1840	2	66.2	½	2½
1841	1	64.3	1	2
1842	0	57.2	3	3
1843	1	50.2	5	6
1844	3	51.1	5	8
1845	5	50.9	5	10
1846	4	54.6	3	7
1847	2	69.3	0	2
1848	0	50.5	1	1
1849	1	44.2	3	4
1850	2	41.8	5	7

[1] 'Low social tension' is indicated by high figures in this index; this series is designed to be plotted inversely.

The business-cycle index is an outgrowth of an extensive history of business fluctuations. Each year is rated from 0 (deep depression) to 5 (major peak). The ratings represent judgements made on the basis of all available statistical evidence, as well as a large body of qualitative material. In addition, an index of business activity was constructed containing some half-dozen of the more significant series. To present that index as a cyclical indicator would have required the abstraction of secular trends from each of the series; the index misrepresented business fluctuations at several points, in the light of wider information. It was thus decided to use the semi-descriptive chart presented here. It is similar in many respects to those compiled from Thorp's *Annals* by Gottfried Haberler (*Prosperity and Depression*). The wheat price is an annual average, derived from weekly quotations (1790–1834) in the *London Gazette* and (after 1834) monthly quotations in the *Gentleman's Magazine*.

The so-called Social Tension Chart is of even more imaginative construction than the business–cycle index. The wheat price was first reduced to a 0 to 5 scale: 0 representing a year of abnormally high wheat price (and thus, like a 0 year in business activity, 'high social tension'), 5 representing a year of abnormally low wheat price. This abstraction of the wheat price was then added to the business–cycle pattern, and the total plotted inversely to a high wheat price and/or estimated severe unemployment thus tending to raise the level of the chart. This method makes the quite arbitrary judgement that cyclical unemployment and high food prices were equally responsible for unrest. Low wheat prices, of course, affected farmers unfavourably and probably, to a lesser extent, agricultural workers. At best, then, the Social Tension Chart summarizes influences operating on the industrial working classes.

It is perhaps unnecessary to emphasize the essentially approximate and descriptive nature of these calculations. They represent, however, a useful summary of a considerable body of evidence, and the results conform fairly well to qualitative political and social data. Intervals of 'high social tension' bred known symptoms of unrest, which, in many cases, expressed themselves in important legislation or in the activities of the Luddites, the Chartists, and other groups: intervals of 'low social tension' saw these movements fade from sight, although the low wheat prices that helped create them often brought the agricultural interests clamouring to Parliament.

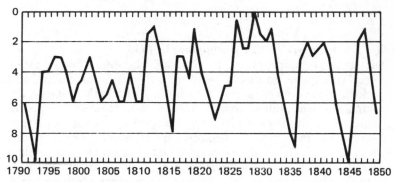

Source: W. W. Rostow, *British Economy of the Nineteenth Century* (Oxford University Press, 1948), pp 123–4

Questions

a   What problems does the historian face when using price and wage indices in the period 1800 to 1850?

b   Do tables 8–11 substantiate Marx's belief that wages will be reduced 'to the same low levels' among the proletariat?

c   Were falling wages the main cause of Chartism?

d   William Cobbett argued that it was difficult 'to agitate a man

with a full stomach'. How far is this assertion borne out by Table
11?

* e 'Chartism was a movement of distress rather than one of
principle.' Discuss.

The final question in this section refers you back to the opening
statement by Professor Court: How far do the tables above 'assist to
define the limits of a problem', in this case Chartism, 'even if they do
not serve to solve it'?

3 Living and Working Conditions

(a) Urban growth (in thousands and percentage growth)

	1801	%	1821	%	1831	%	1841	%	1851
Nottingham	29	37.9	40	25	50	4	52	9.6	57
Manchester	75	68	126	51	182	29.1	235	28.9	303
Oldham	12	83.3	22	45.4	32	34.4	43	23.3	53
Leeds	53	58.5	84	46.4	123	25.2	152	13.2	172
Bradford	13	100.0	26	84.6	44	52.3	67	55.2	104
Halifax	12	41.7	17	29.4	22	27.3	28	21.4	34
Huddersfield	7	85.7	13	46.1	19	31.6	25	24.0	31
Greater London	1,117	43.2	1,600	24.6	1,907	19.2	2,239	17.3	2,685

Source: R. M. Reeve, op cit, pp 203, 205

(b) Mr Pickwick visits Birmingham in 1836

The straggling cottages by the roadside, the dingy hue of every
object visible, the murky atmosphere, the paths of cinders and
brick-dust, the deep red glow of the furnace fires in the distance, the
volumes of dense smoke issuing heavily forth from high toppling
5 chimneys, blackening and obscuring everything around; the glare of
distant lights, the ponderous wagons which toil along the road, laden
with clashing rods of iron, or piled with heavy goods – all betoken
their rapid approach to the great working town of Birmingham.
At they rattled through the narrow thoroughfares leading to the
10 heart of the turmoil, the sights and sounds of earnest occupation
struck more forcibly on the senses. The streets were thronged with
working people. The hum of labour resounded from every house;
lights gleamed from the long casement windows in the attic stories,
and the whirl of wheels and noise of machinery shook the trembling
15 walls. The fires, whose lurid sullen lights had been visible for miles,
blazed fiercely up in the great works and factories of the town. The
din of hammers, the rushing of steam, and the dead heavy clanking
of the engines, was the harsh music which arose from every quarter.

Charles Dickens, *The Pickwick Papers*, Chapter 49

(c) Little Nell visits the Black Country in 1840

... On every side, and as far as the eye can see into the heavy
distance, tall chimneys, crowding on each other, and presenting that
endless repetition of the same dull ugly form, which is the horror of
oppressive dreams, poured out their plague of smoke, obscured the
5   light, and made foul the melancholy air. . . . Men, women and
children, wan in their looks and ragged in attire, tended the engines,
fed their tributary fires, begged upon the road, or scowled half-
naked from the floorless houses. Then came more of the wrathful
monsters, whose like they almost seemed to be in their wildness and
10 their untamed air, screeching and turning round and round again;
and still, before, behind and to the right and left, was the same
interminable perspective of brick towers, never ceasing in their black
vomit, blasting all things living or inanimate, shutting out the face of
day, and closing in on all these horrors with a dense black cloud.
15   By night-time in this dreadful spot! – night, when the smoke
changed to fire, when every chimney spirted up its flame; and places,
that had been dark vaults all day, now shone red-hot, with figures
moving to and fro within their blazing jaws, and calling to one
another with hoarse cries – night, when the noise of every strange
20 machine was aggravated by the darkness; when the people near them
looked wilder and more savage; when bands of unemployed
labourers paraded in the roads, or clustered by torchlight round their
leaders, who told them in stern language of their wrongs . . . night,
which . . . brought with it no peace, nor quiet, nor signs of blessed
25 sleep. . . .

Charles Dickens, *The Old Curiosity Shop*, Chapter 45

(d) Dickens on the impact of the railway

The first shock of a great earthquake had, just at that period, rent the
whole neighbourhood to its centre. Traces of its course were visible
on every side. Houses were knocked down; streets broken through
and stopped; deep pits and trenches dug in the ground; enormous
5 heaps of earth and clay thrown up; buildings that were undermined
and shaking propped by great beams of wood. Here, a chaos of carts,
overthrown and jumbled together, lay topsy-turvy at the bottom of
a steep unnatural hill; there, confused treasures of iron soaked and
rusted in something that had accidentally become a pond. Every-
10 where were bridges that led nowhere; thoroughfares that were
wholly impassable; Babel towers of chimneys, wanting half their
height; temporary wooden houses and enclosures, in the most
unlikely situations; carcases of ragged tenements, and fragments of
unfinished walls and arches, and piles of scaffolding, and wildernes-
15 ses of bricks, and giant forms of cranes, and tripods straddling above
nothing. There were a hundred thousand shapes and substances of
incompleteness, wildly mingled out of their places, upside down,

burrowing in the earth, aspiring in the air, mouldering in the water, and unintelligible as any dream. . . . In short, the yet unfinished and
20 unopened Railroad was in progress. . . .

> Charles Dickens, *Dombey and Son*, first published 1848, Chapter 6 (Penguin edn), pp 120–1

Questions

a Why did the cities and towns in document (a) grow so rapidly between 1801 and 1851?

b Why was Dickens' account of Birmingham in 1836 more optimistic than that of 1840?

c Dickens came from southern England. How fair is it to say, like Francis Klingender, that his attitude in the extracts 'tended to be coloured more and more by his attitude to the social and political struggle'?

d What literary techniques does Dickens use in (c) and (d) to give the impression that the 1840s were 'an age of Despair'? How successful are they in creating images of despair?

* e In his book *Aristocracy and People* Norman Gash writes that

> Had the social novelists really been social thinkers, directing their readers to new and important truths, they would have been producing their books between 1815 and 1825 when the special problems of the industrial working classes were struggling for recognition.

Does this statement cast doubt on the value of Dickens and other contemporary writers as historical sources?

(e) Drinking water and disease

[The River Aire] is charged with the contents of about 200 water closets and similar places, a great number of common drains, the drainings from dung-hills, the Infirmary (dead leeches, poultices for patients etc.), slaughter houses, chemical soap, gas, dung, dyehouses
5 and manufactories, spent blue and black dye, pig manure, old urine wash, with all sorts of decomposed animal and vegetable substances from an extent of drainage . . . amounting to about 30,000,000 gallons per annum of the mass of filth with which the river is charged.

> The *Leeds Intelligencer*, 21 August 1841, quoted in D. Fraser, *The Evolution of the British Welfare State* (Macmillan, 1973), p 53

(f) A European viewpoint

. . . [T]he land is given over to industry's use. The roads which connect the still-disjointed limbs of the great city [Manchester] show, like the rest, every sign of hurried and unfinished work; the

incidental activity of a population bent on gain, which seeks to amass
5   gold so as to have everything else all at once, and, in the interval,
mistrusts all the niceties of life. Some of the roads are paved, but most
of them are full of ruts and puddles into which foot or carriage wheel
sinks deep. Heaps of dung, rubble from buildings, putrid, stagnant
pools are found here and there among the houses and over the
10   bumpy, pitted surfaces of the public places. No trace of the
surveyor's rod or spirit level. . . . On the ground below the level of
the river and overshadowed on every side by immense workshops,
stretches marshy land which widely spaced ditches can neither drain
nor cleanse. Narrow, twisting roads lead to it. They are lined with
15   one-story houses whose ill-fitting planks and broken windows show
them up, even from a distance, as the last refuge a man might find
between poverty and death. . . . Below some of their miserable
dwellings is a row of cellars to which a sunken corridor leads.
Twelve to fifteen human beings are crowded pell-mell into each of
20   these damp, repulsive holes. . . . From this foul drain the greatest
stream of human industry flows out to fertilise the world. From this
filthy sewer pure gold flows. Here humanity attains its most
complete development and its most brutish; here civilization makes
its miracles, and civilized man is turned back almost into a savage.

> Alexis de Tocqueville, *Journeys to England and Ireland*, 1835,
> pp 105–8

(g)   Manchester again

The greatest portion of those districts inhabited by the labouring
population, especially those situated beyond Great Ancoats Street,
are of very recent origin; and from the want of proper police
regulations are untraversed by common sewers. The houses are ill
5   soughed, often ill ventilated, unprovided with privies, and in
consequence, the streets which are narrow, unpaved and worn into
deep ruts, become the common receptacle of mud, refuse and
disgusting ordure. . . .

> Dr J. P. Kay, *The Moral and Physical Condition of the Working
> Classes . . . in Manchester*, 1832, pp 12–13

Questions

a   What were the consequences of lack of adequate sanitation on the
town in the early nineteenth century?
b   What truth is there in de Tocqueville's accusation that in towns
'humanity attains its most complete development and its most
brutish' (lines 22–3 document f)?
c   Using documents (a) to (g) explain what the major problems
were in the nineteenth-century industrial town.
d   Jean Jacques Rousseau wrote that 'men are not made to be
crowded into ant-hills – the more they are crowded together the

more corrupt they will become'. How do these documents support and refute this view?

*   *e*   Is visual evidence of urban conditions in this period more valuable as a historical source than literary evidence? Why should the historian not neglect visual evidence?

(h) Child labour

I have frequently had complaints against myself by the parents of children for beating them. I used to beat them. I am sure that no man can do without it who works long hours; I am sure he cannot. I told them I was very sorry after I had done it, but I was forced to do it.
5 The master expected me to do my work, and I could not do mine unless they did theirs. . . . I have seen them fall asleep, and they have been performing their work with their hands while they were asleep, after the billy had stopped, when their work was over. I have stopped
10 and looked at them for two minutes, going through the motions of piercening fast asleep, when there was really no work to do and they were really doing nothing. . . .

> The evidence of Joseph Badder, a spinner from Leicester, given to the Factory Commission 1833; printed in *Parliamentary Papers*, vol XX, p C 1,19

(i) Cobbett on factories

Some of these lords of the loom have in their employ thousands of miserable creatures. In the cotton-spinning work, these creatures are kept, fourteen hours each day, locked up, summer and winter, in a heat of from eighty to eighty-four degrees. The rules which they are
5 subjected to are such as no negroes were ever subjected to. . . .

> *Political Register*, vol LII, 20 November 1824

(j) Rules!

. . . In some mills, the crime of sitting down to take a little rest is visited with a penalty of one shilling, but let the masters and their rules speak for themselves.

1st. The door of the lodge will be closed ten minutes after the
5 engine starts every morning, and no weaver will afterwards be admitted till breakfast-time. Any weaver who shall be absent during that time shall forfeit three-pence per loom. . . .

9th. All shuttles, brushes, oil cans, wheels, windows etc. if broken, shall be paid for by the weaver.
10 11th. If any hand in the mill is seen talking to another, whistling, or singing, will be fined sixpence.

16th. . . . Any weaver seen from his work during mill hours, will be fined sixpence.

> James Leach, *Stubborn Facts from the Factories by a Manchester*

Operative, published and dedicated to the working classes by William Rathleigh MP, 1844, pp 11–15; quoted in C. McNab and R. Mackenzie, *From Waterloo to the Great Exhibition*, 1982, pp 65–6

(k) The other side of the coin – good employers

The conditions of health in the mills of Turton and Egerton (run by Henry Ashworth) . . . are exceedingly favourable. The working rooms are lofty, spacious and well ventilated, kept at an equable temperature, and scrupulously clean. There is nothing in sight,
5 sound or smell to offend the most fastidious sense.
　　W. C. Taylor, *Notes of a Tour of the Manufacturing Districts of Lancashire*, 1842, pp 22–3

. . . a clean, fresh well ordered house exercises on its inmates a moral no less than a physical influence and has the direct tendency to make the members of a family sober, peaceable and considerate of the feelings and happiness of each other . . . whereas a filthy, squalid and
5 unwholesome dwelling . . . tends directly to make every dweller in such a house selfish and sensual, and the connection is obvious between the constant indulgence of appetite of this class and the formation of habits of dishonesty and violence.
　　E. Akroyd, *On Improved Dwellings for the Working Classes*, 1861, pp 18–19. Akroyd, a Halifax worsted manufacturer, built two 'model' villages for his workers during the 1850s

Questions

a　What were the main problems of working in factories according to this evidence?
b　How true is it that factory reformers in the period up to 1850 over-estimated the extent of abuse in factories?
c　Using documents (k) construct an argument justifying why you as a factory owner had improved conditions for your workers.
*　d　Discuss the proposition that factory reform had a limited effect up to 1850.

4　A Political Dimension

(a) Cobbett on class

. . . the houses which formerly contained little farmers and their happy families are now seen sinking into ruin, all the windows except one or two stopped up, leaving just enough light for some labourer, whose father was, perhaps, a small farmer, to look back
5 upon his half-naked and half-famished children. From his door he surveys all around him the land teeming with the means of luxury to his opulent and overgrown master. . . . We are daily advancing

towards the state in which there are but two classes of men – masters and abject dependents.

Political Register, 15 March 1806

You are for reducing the community into two classes: Masters and Slaves. . . . When master and man were the term everyone was in his place, and all were free. Now, in fact, it is the affair of masters and slaves. . . .

Ibid, 14 April 1821

(b) Response

The middle class have more in common with every other nation in the world than with their own workers who live on their own doorsteps. The workers differ from the middle class in speech, in thoughts and ideas, in customs, morals, politics and religion. . . .

F. Engels, *The Condition of the Working Class in England* (London, 1969), p 52

'Yes,' resumed the younger stranger after a moment's interval. 'Two nations; between whom there is no intercourse and no sympathy; who are as ignorant of each other's habits, thought and feelings, as if they were dwellers in different zones, or inhabitants of different
5   planets; who are formed by a different breeding, are fed by a different food, are ordered by different manners and are not governed by the same laws.'

'You speak of —' said Egremont hesitatingly.

'THE RICH AND THE POOR.'

Benjamin Disraeli, *Sybil or the Two Nations*, 1845 (Oxford University Press edn), p 67

I see two classes dependent on each other in every possible way, yet each evidently regarding the interests of the other as opposed to their own; I never lived in a place before where there were two sets of people always running each other down.

Elizabeth Gaskell, *North and South* (Penguin edn, 1970) p 71

(c) A contrast from 1854

Of all countries Great Britain is the one in which the despotism of capital and the slavery of labour had reached their most advanced stage. [The disappearance of intermediate classes left only] the millionaire commanding whole industrial armies and the wage-slave
5   living only from hand to mouth. . . . In no other country the war between the two classes that constitute modern society has assumed so colossal dimensions and features so distinct and palpable. . . .

Karl Marx; from an article in *The People's Paper*, reprinted in

> *Karl Marx and Frederick Engels on Britain* (Moscow, 1962), p
> 416

The happy balance which characterises England derives from a
recognised hierarchy and a social mobility. . . . Wealth is, to a certain
extent, within the reach of all. Every member of society, whatever
his position, carries in his knapsack the baton of a minister, a general
or a Lord Chancellor. . . . Go on, gentlemen and prosper.

Lord Palmerston

(d) Segregation

Going from the Old Church to Long Millgate [Manchester], the
stroller has at once a row of old fashioned houses at the right, of
which no one has kept its original level; these are remnants of the old
pre-manufacturing Manchester, whose former inhabitants have
5   removed with their descendants into better-built districts and have
left the houses, which were not good enough for them, to a working
class population strongly mixed with Irish blood. Here one is on an
almost undisguised working-men's quarter, for even the shops and
beerhouses hardly take the trouble to exhibit a trifling degree of
10   cleanliness. . . .

> F. Engels, *The Condition of the Working Class in England*, 1844
> (Panther edn, 1972), p 81

Questions

a   What evidence is there in documents (a) to (d) of growing
     working–class consciousness? Why did this occur?
b   How valid were Palmerston's assertions in document (c)?
*   c   To understand the emergence of Chartism what does the
     historian need to understand about the nature of 'class' in the
     early nineteenth century?
d   In what ways did the various authors consider that the working
     class was different from the rest of society?
*   e   Consciousness, yes. Organisation, no. Is this the key to under-
     standing working-class politics and its limited success during the
     first half of the nineteenth century?

(e) Reform in 1832?

. . . When the hungry and angry half-starved labourers complain of
their sufferings, and are ready to break out in acts of violence; will
they be quieted by telling them, that they must not complain *now*, for
they have *got reform*; will they, at the sound of that word, cease to
5   harbour vindictive thoughts relative to those whom they deem their
oppressors? Oh no! the reform must be something more than a *bill*,
something more than a bit of paper, it must, to be productive of

harmony, cause something to be done to *better the state of the people*; and, in order to do this, it must produce and quickly too, not only a change in the management of the affairs of the country, *but a very great change*. . . .

    William Cobbett, *Manchester Lectures*, 1832, p 8

(f) Poor Law reform

I have this bill; but will not now attempt an analysis of it, chiefly because I have not duly considered the extent of all its terrible consequences if attempted to be carried into execution. It is a sort of Austrian project: a scheme for bringing every thing and every body within the control, the immediate control, of the kingly part of Government. . . . I have talked to twenty gentlemen, farmers and attorneys; every man of them has said: 'If this bill be attempted to be put into execution, there will be a revolution in England'. . . .

    William Cobbett, *Political Register*, 3 May 1834

. . . Half-a-dozen counties are in a state of partial commotion; the jails are opening the doors to receive those who are called the rebels against the Poor-Law bill. No matter as to any other thing relative to this measure; here is the country disturbed; here are the jails filling; here are wives and children screaming after their fathers; here are the undeniable facts. . . .

    Ibid, 13 June 1835

And if this damnable law, which violated all the laws of God, was continued, and all means of peacably putting an end to it had been made in vain, then, in the words of their banner, 'For children and wife we'll war to the knife'. If the people who produce all wealth could not be allowed, according to God's word, to have the kindly fruits of the earth which they had, in obedience to God's Word, raised by the sweat of their brow, then war to the knife with their enemies, who were the enemies of God. If the musket and the pistol, the sword and the pike were of no avail, let the women take the scissors, the child the pin and the needle. If all failed, then the firebrand – aye, the firebrand – the firebrand, I repeat. The palace shall be in flames. . . .

    From a speech given by J. R. Stephens at Newcastle; printed in *Northern Star*, 6 January 1838

(g) To Chartism

I believe that nothing will ever be done to relieve the distress of the working classes, unless they take it into their own hands. With these views I left England, and with these views I am returned.

    George Loveless, *The Victims of Whiggery*, 1837, printed in T. Barker (ed), *The Long March of Everyman 1750–1960*

(Penguin edn, 1978), p 100. Loveless was one of the Tolpuddle Martyrs who had been transported to Australia but returned in 1837

The settled conviction of the Chartists was that bad trade, dear living, and all their misfortunes rose from bad laws, and that if only they could get votes and send men of their own to Parliament they would so order matters that a reign of peace and plenty would at once be inaugurated.
F. Peel, *The Rising of the Luddites, Chartists and Plugdrawers* (2nd edn, Heckmondwike, 1888), p 328

Questions

a Why was the 1832 reform insufficient according to Cobbett in document (e)? What justification was there for working-class criticism of the Reform Act?

b Was the 1834 Poor Law Amendment Act an 'Austrian project'? Why did it not lead to revolution in England?

* *c* Opposition like that of Stephens to the new poor law was as moral in content as those who were attempting to implement it. It was just that their views of morality differed. Discuss this dilemma.

d Using the two documents in (g) debate the proposition that Chartism was a response to poor conditions which only political change could resolve successfully.

Further work

a The labouring population identified with their locality and its problems rather than with national issues. Does this explain the relative failure of working-class movements in the period up to 1838?

b Politics of 'distress' or politics of principle? Discuss in relation to working class radicalism in the early nineteenth century.

c The impact of economic change was never a black or white issue. Have historians misunderstood this?

d Was there a working class in 1838?

e The historian should try to be objective in his discussion of the past. Is this possible in relation to the Industrial Revolution and its effects?

II   The Initial Surge 1836–39

Demands for political reform by the working classes were not exhausted with the 'betrayal' of 1832. Working-class agitation may have been diverted into factory reform, trade unionism and from 1835 into anti-poor law protest. *But* the failure to achieve 'ten hours', the government prosecution of the Tolpuddle labourers, the debacle of the Grand National Consolidated Trades Union and the worsening economic conditions brought parliamentary reform back to the top of the agenda. Working-class radicals argued that until working people – by which they generally meant men – had the vote and could elect their own Parliament no reform beneficial to them would be passed. This chapter examines the responses that were Chartism between 1836 and 1839, a period of intense slump in the newly expanded industrial areas.

The objectives of Chartism are examined in the first section, from the aims of the London Working Men's Association of 1836 through Bronterre O'Brien's statement to the six points of the Charter itself. These objectives are central to an understanding of the Chartist movement since they were the *one* thing on which the variety of Chartists could agree. But was Mr Doubtful correct in agreeing that they seemed to be quite reasonable?

Chartists may well have agreed over the Charter but they were perennially unable to agree on the *means* whereby these ends should be achieved. The various methods which they employed are studied in the middle section. Associations? District meetings? Large-scale demonstrations like those at Peep Green? Oratory? Demagogy? The Press? All are considered in the documents just as they were by contemporaries. *But*, as the third section illustrates, the diversity, the variety of response and solution, the illusory nature of the authority of the Convention when faced by the reality of the power of Government, even O'Connor, that advocate of physical force – or was he? – counselling caution about the meetings at the Bull Ring in Birmingham, showed the inconsistencies of the movement. Perhaps it was because Chartism was only a message of hope, a millenarian dream, that it was to fail in its early years. Most Chartists were not willing to fight, to destroy and then reshape. There was a logical connection between the Convention and Parliament: both represented constitutional authority; for Chartists that was the problem.

1 Aims and Objectives

(a) The objects of the London Working Men's Association 1836

The objects of the Association were the following:

1. To draw into one bond of unity the intelligent and influential portion of the working classes in town and country.

2. To seek by every legal means to place all classes of society in possession of their equal political and social rights.

3. To devise every possible means, and to use every exertion, to remove those cruel laws that prevent the free circulation of thought through the medium of a cheap and honest press.

4. To promote, by all available means, the education of the rising generation, and the extirpation of those systems which tend to future slavery. . . .

7. To publish their views and sentiments in such form and manner as shall best serve to create a moral, reflecting, yet energetic public opinion; so as eventually to lead to a gradual improvement in the condition of the working classes, without violence or commotion. . . .

> William Lovett, *Life and Struggles*, R. H. Tawney (ed), 1920, pp 94–5

(b) Bronterre O'Brien's views January 1837

. . . the end I have in view is social equality for all and each, to obtain this we must first have political equality for each and all. To obtain political equality, we must have a more extensive and effective organization of the working classes, and of that portion of the middle class which is immediately dependent on their custom, than has hitherto been even thought of, much less accomplished. It will, therefore, be an object of mine to promote such extensive and effective organization, and as the best means of promoting it, I will never cease to recommend and encourage, among those classes, knowledge and union; a full and accurate knowledge of their wrongs and of their rights; and a steady union of purpose to redress the one and obtain permanent enjoyment of the other.

> *Bronterre's National Reformer*, 7 January 1837

(c) The meeting at the Crown and Anchor 28 February 1837

. . . Four thousand democrats, at least, were present at the meeting. The immense room of the Crown and Anchor was crowded to overflowing, several hundreds stood outside on the corridors and the stairs, or went away for want of accommodation. The platform was equally crammed as the body of the room, and notwithstanding the great pressure and the great excitement that prevailed, the most perfect order characterised the whole of the proceedings from beginning to end.

The meeting . . . was convened by the Working Men's Associa-
10 tion to petition for a reform of Parliament, based on the five cardinal
points of Radicalism, viz: UNIVERSAL SUFFRAGE, EQUAL REPRE-
SENTATION, ANNUAL PARLIAMENTS, VOTE BY BALLOT and NO
PROPERTY QUALIFICATION FOR MEMBERS. . . . [Mr Vincent] . . .
spoke with boldness, fluency and a perfect command of his subject.
15 Paine is evidently a great favourite with him. . . . Among other good
things, he gave a masterly exposition of the 'rotten House of
Commons', and a capital spicy hash of Paine's exposure of Black-
stone's old humbug about the checks of our 'nicely balanced
Constitution'. Sir Bobby Peel also came in for a lash or two, in
20 consequence of his late audacious harangue at Glasgow in which he
described the American system of government as the despotism of a
majority. . . . [Mr. Hoare] . . . instituted a comparison between the
relative knowledge of the aristocracy, middle and working classes, in
which he showed with unanswerable truth that with all their
25 pretended superiority, the two former classes are, after all, vastly
inferior to the working classes in all those departments of knowledge
which society most needs, and without which it could not exist an
hour. . . . 'They pretend', said one of the speakers 'that our ignorance
is the sole cause of their excluding us – odious hypocrisy! It is our
30 knowledge, not our ignorance they fear. If we were really ignorant,
they would give us the franchise, as they did to the poor 40/-
freeholders in Ireland. . . .

Bronterre O'Brien's account printed in the *London Mercury*, 4
March 1837

(d) What Chartists attacked!

What a farce the present system is! The present House of Commons
does not represent the people, but only those fellows who live by
profits and usury – a rascally crew who have no interest in the real
welfare of the country. Pawnbrokers are enfranchised, and two
5 thousand brothel-owners in London all have votes, but honest folk
have none. Not a single stockbroker is without a vote, yet there is not
a man among them who does not deserve the gallows. Every lawyer
in the country can vote – every thief of them – yet when did any one
of this gang add a stiver to the wealth of the nation? . . . Votes have
10 been given to all the parsons, who live by explaining those things
which they tell us are inexplicable, who preach abnegation of the
lusts of the flesh while losing no opportunities of greasing their own
rosy gills. . . . Then you have those slaughtering, soldier-flogging,
billiard-playing creatures called officers of the army, and the
15 cotton-lords who possess all the skill and trickery and daring and
effrontery of the pick-pocket, the burglar and the highwayman
rolled into one – they all have votes, but not the working people. It is,
indeed, disgusting to see how much of the honey is appropriated by

the drones, and what a pittance is left to the bees of the hive; and how
20 the parliamentary franchise is monopolised by one-tenth of the
population – and that tenth the worst tenth.

From a speech of Bronterre O'Brien reported in *Charter*, 14
April 1839

Questions

a Using the four extracts, explain what the objectives of the
Chartists were in the years 1836 and 1837.

b To what were the Chartists opposed?

c In what ways were the objectives of the London Working Men's
Association different from those put forward at the Crown and
Anchor meeting in early 1837? Account for these differences.

* d In emphasising educational objectives Lovett misread the mood
of the working classes and their demands for political emancipation. Discuss.

e Why were the views of Tom Paine discussed by Mr Vincent
(document c) of such influence upon radical thinking?

f Was Chartism a political movement first and a social movement
second?

(e) The Charter itself

THE SIX POINTS OF THE PEOPLE'S CHARTER.

1. A VOTE for every man twenty-one years of age, of sound mind,
and not undergoing punishment for crime.

2. THE BALLOT – To protect the elector in the exercise of his vote.

5   3. NO PROPERTY QUALIFICATION for Members of Parliament –
thus enabling the constituencies to return the man of their choice, be
he rich or poor.

4. PAYMENT OF MEMBERS, thus enabling an honest tradesman,
working man, or other person, to serve a constituency, when taken
10   from his business to attend to the interests of the Country.

5. EQUAL CONSTITUENCIES, securing the same amount of representation for the same number of electors, instead of allowing small
constituencies to swamp the votes of large ones.

6. ANNUAL PARLIAMENTS, thus presenting the most effectual
15   check to bribery and intimidation, since though a constituency
might be bought once in seven years (even with the ballot), no purse
could buy a constituency (under a system of universal suffrage) in
each ensuing twelve-month; and since members, when elected for a
year, would not be able to defy and betray their constituents as now.

20   Subjoined are the names of the gentlemen who embodied these
principles into the document called the 'People's Charter' at an
influential meeting held at the British Coffee House, London, on the
7th of June 1837:

Daniel O'Connell, Esq., M.P.   Mr Henry Hetherington.

John Arthur Roebuck, Esq., M.P.   Mr John Cleave.
John Temple Leader, Esq., M.P.   Mr James Watson.
Charles Hindley, Esq., M.P.   Mr Richard Moore.
Thomas Perronet Thompson, Esq.,   Mr William Lovett.
   M.P.   Mr Henry Vincent.
William Sharman Crawford Esq.,
   M.P.

> F. C. Mather (ed), *Chartism and Society*; an anthology of documents (London, 1981), pp 46–7

Questions

a What were the justifications put forward in the People's Charter for the Six Points?

b Why were the six MPs willing to sign a document calling for radical political change? Who were they?

* c The Charter contained the traditional demands of political radicals since the seventeenth century. To understand Chartism and its failure it is necessary to examine this tradition. Discuss this issue critically.

(f) The manifesto of the Chartist Convention made public 14 May 1839

We respectfully submit the following propositions for your serious consideration:

That at all the simultaneous public meetings to be held for the purpose of petitioning the Queen to call good men to her councils, as
5 well as at all subsequent meetings of your unions and associations, up to the 1st of July, you submit the following questions to the people there assembled:

1. Whether they will be prepared, at the request of the Convention, to withdraw all sums of money they may individually or
10 collectively have placed in savings banks, private banks, or in the hands of any person hostile to their just rights?

2. Whether, at the same request, they will be prepared immediately to convert all their paper money into gold and silver?

3. Whether, if the Convention shall determine that a sacred month
15 will be necessary to prepare the millions to secure the charter of their political salvation, they will firmly resolve to abstain from their labours during that period, as well as from the use of all intoxicating drink?

4. Whether, according to their old constitutional right – a right
20 which modern legislators would fain annihilate – they have prepared themselves with the arms of freemen to defend the laws and the constitutional privileges their ancestors bequeathed to them?

5. Whether they will provide themselves with chartist candidates, so as to be prepared to propose them for their representatives at the

25 next general election; and, if returned by a show of hands, such
candidates to consider themselves veritable representatives of the
people – to meet in London at a time hereafter to be determined on?
        6. Whether they will resolve to deal exclusively with Chartists,
and in all cases of persecution rally round and protect all those who
30 may suffer in their righteous cause?
        7. Whether by all and every means in their power, they will
perseveringly contend for the great objects of the People's Charter,
and resolve that no counter agitation for a less measure of justice shall
divert them from their righteous object?
35   8. Whether the people will determine to obey all the just and
constitutional requests of the majority of the Convention?
        Printed in D. Jones, *Chartism and the Chartists* (London, 1975),
        pp 58–9

Questions

a   In what ways does this Manifesto show that the Chartists had
    great regard for the Constitution? Why was this so?
b   What methods does the Manifesto suggest might be used to
    achieve political freedom? Would you call these revolutionary?
c   In what ways does this document demonstrate that Chartism
    was concerned with human rights?
*   d   The Chartists' dilemma in 1839 was that they were trying to
    obtain a revolutionary goal by constitutional means. This is why
    they failed. Discuss.

(g) The Chartists were called ugly names, the swinish multitude
unwashed and levellers. I never knew levelling advocated amongst
the Chartists, neither in public nor in private, for they did not believe
in it, nor have I known a case of plunder in the town, though
5   thousands have marched through its streets to meetings in various
places. What they wanted was a voice in making the laws they were
called upon to obey; they believed that taxation without representation was tyranny, and ought to be resisted; they took a leading part in
agitating in favour of the ten hour question, the repeal of the taxes on
10 knowledge, education, co-operation, civil and religious liberties and
the land question, for they were the true pioneers in all the great
movements of their time.
        Benjamin Wilson, 'The Struggles of an Old Chartist' pub-
        lished 1887 and reprinted in D. Vincent (ed), *Testaments of
        Radicalism* (London, 1977), p 210

(h) Mr. Doubtful What are the benefits you anticipate from the
adoption of the Charter?
        Radical. The repeal of bad laws and the making of good laws in
their stead; a reduction of taxation, by which the productive industry

5 of the nation would be increased; the abolition of the enormous
   abuses of the civil and criminal law, which amount in most cases to
   an utter denial of justice to the poor; a liberal and general system of
   national education, without reference to sect or creed, which would
   tend at once to diminish crime, by striking at its root. The cost of the
10 civil and criminal justice in this country is above two millions, while
   only 30,000*l* is devoted to national education. Would it not be far
   better to diminish the former amount by increasing the latter? . . .

> From a tract issued by the Finsbury Tract Society 1839, called
> 'The Question "What is a Chartist?" Answered'; printed in
> D. Thompson (ed), *The Early Chartists* (London, 1971), pp
> 89–94

Questions

a What did the Radical think would be the result of adopting the
     Charter?
b What does Benjamin Wilson mean by 'levelling'? How valid do
     you think his assertion that the Chartists were not levellers really
     is?
c How reasonable were Chartist demands in the 1830s?

Using all the documents in this section answer the question: What
was a Chartist?

2 Methods

Associations and meetings

(a) Early in 1839 our association joined the Staffordshire Potteries
district, and, by the payment of a small weekly subscription to it, we
had the privilege of lecturers being sent to us for open-air meetings.
The first of these was held on Snow Hill on Monday, April 8th. 1839.
5 I, together with Robinson, my brother Charles, and three or four of
my brother bandsmen (the remainder of the band being Tory
Churchmen), played before the lecturer, Mr John Richards, and a
large muster of working people, from the Swan Inn, Pillory Street,
to the place of meeting. There was a large and attentive audience, and
10 Mr Richards explained the principles of the People's Charter to the
satisfaction of all present. Thus ended our first open-air Chartist
meeting. We afterwards held open-air meetings in Wood Street in
the evening, once or twice a week and also on Sunday evenings, all
[addressed by] local speakers and readers of articles and speeches
15 from the Star, including the Rev. J. R. Stephens' sermons against the
New Poor Law. On Sunday evenings hymns were sung and Mr
William Cooper delivered a Chartist sermon. Weekly meetings were
held in our workshop; there were no political beer-and-billiards club
houses in Chartist days. . . .

Thomas Dunning, 'Reminiscences'; printed in D. Vincent (ed), op cit, p 135

(b) Joseph Wilson, my uncle, was a small piece-maker in the village and it was about this time that I went to help him in the warehouse, and wind bobbins. My aunt was a famous politician, a Chartist, and a great admirer of Fergus O'Connor. It was whilst there that I first
5 became acquainted with the Chartist movement [in Halifax]. The delegates to the convention broke up at Whitsuntide and forthwith addressed meetings throughout the country. On Whit-Monday 1839, a great meeting was held at Peep Green, which I attended along with Samuel Jackson, a neighbour; we joined the procession in
10 Halifax which was a very large one headed by a band of music, and marched by Godley Lane and Hipperholme, at which place the Queensbury procession joined us; on reaching the top of the hill above Bailiffe Bridge we met the Bradford procession, headed by Peter Bussey, on horseback, and wearing a green sash. On our arrival
15 at the place of the meeting some thousands of people had already assembled, and for almost an hour we witnessed the continuous arrival of processions from different directions, with bands playing and flags and banners flying, a great many of them far superior to any that I have seen in our late demonstrations. . . . The proceedings
20 opened with prayers by Mr William Thornton, at the close of which Fergus O'Connor put his hands on his shoulders and said 'Well done, Thornton, when we get the Charter I will see that you are made Archbishop of York.' . . . This was my first meeting in the Chartist movement.

Benjamin Wilson, 'The Struggles of an Old Chartist', ibid, pp 197–8

(c) On Saturday evening, a large number of the disciples of the lamented Henry Hunt, met at the house of Mr Abraham Matley . . . to commemorate the birthday of that great man. The room was tastefully hung with the portraits of political characters, at the head
5 of which was a large painting of Peterloo, with the black flag waving over it, and this inscription in characters of blood: – 'Ashton demands Universal Suffrage or Universal Vengeance'. . . . After opening the business he [Mr Ralph Clough] concluded a very neat address by calling on all present to follow the dictates of our late
10 departed friend. The Chairman gave 'The people, the only source of power'. . . . Song by Mr. Andrews – 'Peterloo'. The chairman then gave 'The immortal memory of Henry Hunt, the man who never deceived the people', which was drunk in solemn silence, the company up-standing and uncovered. . . . The Chairman next gave
15 'the Plaintiffs in Prison, and Defendants at large' . . . 'the healths of Frost, Williams and Jones, and may they soon be restored to their country and families'. . . . The evening getting very late, the

Chairman next proposed, 'The immortal memory of Thomas Paine, Robert Emmett, William Cobbett, Cartwright, Sydney, Tyler,
20 Hampden, Elihu Palmer, the blind philosopher, Volney, Voltaire, Mirabeau, Muir, Washington, Tell, Hofer, Wallace, Joshua Hobson, and all the illustrious dead of every nation, who by their acts or deeds have contributed to the cause of freedom'. . . . A vote of thanks being given to the Chairman and three cheers for Feargus O'Connor, three
25 for Frost, Williams and Jones, three groans for the Whigs and Peterloo butchers, and three times three for the Charter, the meeting broke up at a very late hour, all present being highly gratified with the evening's entertainment.

Description of a Chartist club celebration at Ashton-under-Lyne in November 1840; printed in D. Jones, op cit, pp 78–9

Questions

a What information can you extract from these documents about the way in which Chartism was organised in the industrial North?

b David Jones argues that 'The public meeting was *the* Chartist experience. . . . It brought humour, colour and a sense of community to their lives . . .'. How do documents (a) and (b) demonstrate this?

c Why is the list of people to whom a toast was proposed in document (c) (lines 18–23) important? What value does it have in placing Chartism in its context?

d Why did the Whigs get 'three groans' (c, line 25)?

* e What role did the public house play in the early developments of Chartism?

The press

(d) . . . [Joshua] Hobson, Mr [William] Hill and others in Yorkshire, seeing the want of a newspaper as an organ for the rising movement, had succeeded in raising some few hundreds of pounds by shares to establish one. O'Connor persuaded them that they would not be able
5 to get the necessary amount, and that the mixed authority of a committee would hamper the editor and render the paper inefficient. He proposed that the shareholders should lend him the money already raised, for which he would guarantee interest, and that he would find the rest of the capital and commence the paper at once,
10 that Hobson should be the publisher and Hill editor. This was done. It was entitled the Northern Star. But there is every reason to believe that at that time he had no capital, and that the money of the shareholders was the only money ever invested in the paper. Fortunately for him it soon rose to a very large circulation, reaching
15 at last to some 60,000 a week, and when, during Frost's trial, he gave

one week's profits to the defence fund he handed over £200 as that week's profit. Thus the Star at once gave him and his party a general influence, while the sayings and doings of his special favourites were regularly reported and eulogised. . . .

From Robert Lowery, 'Passages in the Life of a Temperance Lecturer'; printed in B. Harrison and P. Hollis (eds), *Robert Lowery: Radical and Chartist* (London, 1979), p 124

(e) The formation of political unions was only a part of the machinery necessary for carrying out a great popular movement. It would have been of little use to call the people together if no organ had existed to enforce their claims or give a record of their
5 proceedings. It was, therefore, a matter of necessity for the radical party to establish a press through which the public might be supplied with information on all the subjects relating to the common cause.

The London Working Men's Association already possessed its journal. When the law which imposed a fourpenny stamp upon
10 newspapers was repealed, Hetherington's Twopenny Despatch changed its name to the London Despatch. . . . Its policy was that of what was called the moral force party, who disclaimed all idea of seeking a change by physical force. . . . Its articles were generally of a mild persuasive tone. Another paper was launched in the borough of
15 Leeds under the title of the Northern Star. Its proprietor was the popular Feargus O'Connor who had become the idol of the operatives in the manufacturing districts. Never was a journal started more opportunely. It caught and reflected the spirit of the times. It was not, however, with his own means alone that O'Connor
20 succeeded in establishing the Star. Not less than £800 was subscribed in shares by his friends, without whose timely assistance it is doubtful whether he could, at that time, have ventured on the speculation. Those friends had faith in its success, and the result proved the reasonableness of their anticipations, for the Northern
25 Star speedily stood at the head of the democratic journals. Its editor was the Rev. William Hill, an acute and clever but not a very agreeable writer. It was not, however, for its editorial department that it was so much valued. Two circumstances contributed to raise it in popular estimation. One of these was the popularity of O'Connor,
30 a popularity which was largely due to the fact of his having a journal in which to record all his proceedings and to place his words and deeds in the most advantageous light. The other circumstance was, that the Star was regarded as the most complete record of the movement. There was not a meeting held in any part of the country,
35 in however remote a spot, that was not reported in its columns, accompanied by all the flourishes calculated to excite an interest in the reader's mind, and to inflate the vanity of the speakers. . . . Thus men of very mediocre abilities appeared to people at a distance to be oracles of political wisdom. . . .

R. C. Gammage, *History of the Chartist Movement 1837–1854*,
2nd edn, 1894, pp 17–18

Questions

a In what ways do the accounts of the founding of the *Northern Star*
by Robert Lowery and R. C. Gammage differ? Why do you think
this is so?

b Why was the *Northern Star* so important for Feargus O'Connor?

* c 'When the Press is free, the people will know their rights.'
Discuss this statement in relation to the press and Chartism.

d Why was a free press so important to the Chartists?

Demagogy

(f) Next to this fault was the disposition [among the leaders] to
quarrel. But quarrelling was almost inevitable when not one man,
but many men, desired to become dictators. It was almost equally
inevitable when such a man as Feargus O'Connor, who had few of
5 the qualities of a powerful leader save extraordinary force of
character, had acquired absolute dominion over the cause. . . . The
ascendancy of Feargus O'Connor would have been unaccountable
but for the fact that he owned the Northern Star. . . . Through it
Feargus every week addressed a letter to his followers – 'the blistered
10 hands and unshorn chins of the working classes'. The letter was
generally as full of claptrap as it was bestrewn with words and
sentences in capital type. But the turgid claptrap took. The people of
that period seemed to relish denunciation, and O'Connor gave them
plenty of it. Blatant in print, he was equally blatant on the platform.
15 More of a demagogue than a democrat, he was fond of posing as the
descendant of Irish kings. 'Never a man of my order,' he was in the
habit of declaring, 'has devoted himself as I have done to the working
classes'. It was his delight, too, to boast that he had 'never travelled a
mile or eaten a meal at the people's expinse.' He even claimed in 1851
20 that he had spent £130,000 in the cause of the Charter. It pleased the
working people to hear themselves addressed as 'Fustian Jackets',
'Old Guards' and 'Imperial Chartists'. Nor did it displease them
when their leader assumed a royal title and called himself 'Feargus
Rex'. . . . It was considered curious that Feargus's visits to towns in
25 the provinces generally synchronized with the appearance in the
same towns of a lady who was then a star in the theatrical world. This
lady was Mrs Nisbett. . . . O'Connor himself does not seem to have
made much secrecy of the relations between himself and the
actress. . . . The alliance, such as it was, was probably consecrated by
30 some measure of affection, since it was stated that the lady, when
O'Connor had to be removed to a lunatic asylum, left the stage and
nursed and tended him as long as he lived.

    The common notion of O'Connor outside the ranks of his

personal followers was that he was a charlatan and a humbug – an
35 adventurer who traded on the passions of the people for his own
profit and advantage. A correcter notion would have been that he
was a victim of his own delusions. . . .

> W. E. Adams, *Memoirs of a Social Atom* (London, 1903), pp
> 203–5, 208–9

(g) After listening attentively for half an hour there gradually arose a
visible restlessness among the whole mass. O'Connor had reported
on this and that, and then there followed his disquisition, and he was
advancing into the heart of his subject. He had already several times
5 audibly slammed the edge of the rostrum with his right hand, several
times he had stamped his foot more and more angrily and shaken his
head more wildly. He made preparation to attack the enemy – the
meeting noticed this and spurred him on by loud clapping – it was a
red rag to a bull. Then the Titan had gripped his victim! The voice
10 took on a louder and fuller sound, the sentences became shorter, they
were wrung in spasms from his seething breast, the fist drummed
more wildly against the edge of the rostrum, the face of the orator
became pale, his limbs trembled, the cataract of his rage had flooded
over the last barrier, and onwards thundered the floodtide of his
15 eloquence, throwing down all before it, breaking up and smashing
everything in its way – and I do believe that the man would have
talked himself to death if he had not been interrupted by an applause
which shook the whole house and set it vibrating.

> From an account of O'Connor in action by George Weerth, a
> young German exile; printed in D. Jones, op cit, p 104

(h) . . . What was the position in which the working classes stood?
Why, they were Nature's children, and all they wanted was Nature's
produce. They had been told to stand by the old constitution. Why,
that was the constitution of tallow and wind. The people wanted the
5 railroad constitution, the gas constitution, but they did not want
Lord Melbourne and his tallow constitution; neither did they want
Lord Melbourne and his fusty laws. What they wanted was a
constitution and laws of a railroad genius, propelled by a steam
power and enlightened by the rays of gas. They wanted a Legislature
10 who had the power as well as the inclination to advance after the
manner he had just pointed out. They wanted that the science of
legislation should not stand still. The people had only to show the
present House of Commons that they were determined and its
reform must take place. . . . He counselled them against all rioting,
15 all civil wars; but still, in the hearing of the House of Commons, he
would say that, rather than see the people oppressed, rather than see
the constitution violated, while the people were in daily want, if no
man would do so, if the constitution were violated, he would himself
lead the people to death or glory. . . .

Record of a speech made on 17 September 1838 in the Palace Yard, Westminster and printed in W. E. Adams, op cit, pp 205–7

Questions

a   What reliability can the historian place upon W. E. Adams as a source on O'Connor?

b   Using these three extracts account for O'Connor's success as an orator.

c   What evidence is there in these extracts that O'Connor had a positive programme of reform?

*   d   Was O'Connor 'a victim of his own delusions' (document f, line 37)?

e   'We know not of a more decidedly useful and patriotic body of men at the present time than this.' (The *Northern Star*, February 1842). Account for the role of the lecturer and missionary in the Chartist movement.

3   Conventions and Riots

This section does not deal with the Newport rising, which was certainly the most publicised Chartist attempt at direct action and is dealt with more fully in Chapter 3.

(a)   The Convention of 1839

It was now determined that instead of local petitions for the Charter there should be one general or national one – each district to gather and send in signatures to it, and that as many districts as could should, after due notice, elect a representative, or representatives, to
5   a national convention to meet in London on the day on which the Government might announce the assembling of Parliament for 1839. That the duty of this convention should be to present this petition to the House of Commons and urge its support on the members of that House. Every district was expected to contribute to a fund for the
10   general expense of the convention. . . . During the autumn of 1838 a public meeting was held in the open air to elect delegates for the Newcastle district. The different associations of the district had been consulted as to the number of members to be elected. . . . The choice fell upon Dr. John Taylor, of Ayrshire, in Scotland, and Julian
15   Harney of London, along with myself. . . . The General Convention of the Industrious Classes met at the British Coffee House, Cockspur Street, Charing-cross on Monday morning, at 10 a.m., 4th. February 1839. Mr. William Lovett was unanimously chosen to be secretary. The members then handed in their credentials of election, and it was
20   found that there were 53 present. Several others arrived during the week. . . . Now that we were fairly installed . . . the individuality of

the members became more marked, as well as the divisions of party. Some could think for themselves, and at once gave utterance to their own opinions. Others were pledged to O'Connor and deemed him
25   their leader. . . . On 11 March 1839 a crowded meeting was held at the Crown and Anchor, Strand . . . when O'Connor, Harney and others spoke in the strongest language, and uged the people to be prepared for the coming struggle . . . and speedily after Messrs. Salt, Hadly and Douglas of Birmingham, tendered their resignation as
30   members of the convention. . . . It was determined to adjourn to Birmingham, where the Convention would be in the heart of the country and surrounded by a population amongst the most enthusiastic of its supporters, and it adjourned to Birmingham on May 13th. . . .
Robert Lowery, printed in B. Harrison and P. Hollis (eds), op cit, pp 117–19, 127–8, 135

(b)   Apathy in London

All the members with the exception of the London delegates, were ignorant of the state of political feeling of the metropolis, and even the delegates themselves were far from agreed upon it. It is certain that London had given no evidence of being alive to the importance
5   of the move now made, its character was that of having sent more delegates worse paid, fewer signatures, less rent and held smaller meetings, in proportion than any district in England or Scotland, which returned a member to the Convention. It was of the utmost consequence that its real state of feeling should be known, as many
10   thought that no movement could be effectual in which the capital did not take a most decided and active interest, if not a part.
Doctor John Taylor, writing of the first session of the Convention later in the year in the *Northern Star*, 9 November 1839

(c)   At Birmingham

. . . the Convention re-assembled at Birmingham . . . on Monday 1st July. The first subject which engaged the attention of that body was the removal of itself to London. . . . The subject of a National Defence Fund was then put forward . . . [O'Connor] then said that
5   they ought to advise the people of their right of possessing arms and gave an account of a trial at Mansfield, in which he had attended to prosecute several shopkeepers, who had been training and drilling with arms. . . . This led to a discussion on the propriety of the people continuing their meetings in the Bull Ring. . . . The Convention was
10   now the only constituted authority in the country and [O'Connor] thought they should not press the power which was in their hands too suddenly upon the people. It had now gained a great importance

in the country, and it would not be well to hazard a general defeat by
gaining a sectional triumph. . . .

R. C. Gammage, op cit, pp 123, 126–7

(d)   The Bull Ring Riots

The following are the circumstances that led to my arrest, and that of
my fellow prisoner Mr. Collins: – It appears that the middle classes
of Birmingham, during the agitation for the Reform Bill, were in the
habit of meeting in the Bull-ring, in conjunction with the working
5   classes, during a portion of their dinner hours and in the evenings, for
the purpose of hearing the news of the day; when stirring appeals
from the newspapers were read, and speeches made regarding the
matters before Parliament. . . . When, . . . the agitation for the
People's Charter commenced, following the example of their former
10   leaders, the working classes began to hold their meetings also in the
Bull-ring. But this of course was not to be endured by the ex-reform
authorities; what was once right and legal in themselves was
denounced as seditious and treasonable in the multitude. The poor
infatuated workers, however, could not perceive the distinction of
15   the Birmingham authorities between the two political measures, but
continued to meet as usual. . . . At last the governing powers of
Birmingham . . . sent to London to their former friends and allies
requesting them to send down a strong posse of the new police to
assist them. They came down by rail, and were no sooner out of their
20   vans than they were led on by the authorities, truncheon in hand, and
commenced a furious attack upon the men, women and children
who were assembled in the Bull-ring, listening peacefully to a person
reading a newspaper. This proceeding, as may be supposed, greatly
exasperated the people. . . . The morning after this brutal attack, a
25   number of the working classes of Birmingham called at the
Convention Room. . . . Feeling most strongly with them, that a
great injustice had been inflicted, I drew up and proposed to the
Convention the three following resolutions. . . .

1st. – That this Convention is of the opinion that a wanton, flagrant
and unjust outrage has been made upon the people of Birmingham
by a bloodthirsty and unconstitutional force from London. . . .
2nd. – That the people of Birmingham are the best judge of their
own right to meet in the Bull-ring or elsewhere. . . .
3rd. – That the summary and despotic arrest of Dr. Taylor . . .
affords another convincing proof of the absence of all justice in
England and clearly shows that there is no security of life, liberty
or property till the people have some control over the laws which
they are called upon to obey. . . .

Mr Collins and myself were next arrested. . . .

William Lovett, op cit, pp 221–3

(e) 'The Sacred Month'

... The boasting and exaggeration of the general strength had been believed by many individuals. The multitude took language for facts, and expected them to be realised; while the leaders, becoming more perfectly acquainted with the facts of the whole country, were
5   forced to change their ideas, they still used the same language. They had not the moral courage to say – 'We have been wrong. . . .' . . . Strange inconsistency and perversion of judgement appeared in some of the members who had come first as prudent moral force men. They now became mostly reckless and violent in language.
10 Those like Dr. Taylor . . . became more braggart and violent in expression, evidently wishing it to be inferred that the failure in attaining immediate redress was because the rest of the Convention did not possess the courage which they did. The 'National Holiday' or 'sacred month' of cessation from all labour, was an idea which the
15 Birmingham men had. Whatever might have been meant by it at first, it meant in the people's minds the chances of a physical contest; not an insurrection or assault on the authorities but that by retiring from labour . . . they would so derange the whole country that the authorities would endeavour to coerce them back, and that they
20 would resist the authorities unless their rights were conceded, and thus bring the struggle to an issue.

R. Lowery, cited in B. Harrison and P. Hollis (eds), op cit, p 142

(f) The debacle – the Convention ends

There was evidently a conviction that the national holiday could not be kept, but a total lack of conviction amongst the leading men to say so. Dr. McDowell and others still wanted to recommend it. He was wont to boast of the thousands of armed men in Lancashire, and P.
5   Bussy, the Bradford delegate, would often boast of 10,000 armed men there; yet, on close examination, Dr. M. admitted that if he named 400 armed men for his neighbourhood he would probably overstate the number. With one or two exceptions, none of the delegates could say their districts were prepared, and the vast force
10 was found only to exist in imaginative rant. The Convention passed a resolution stating what they had done to attain the Charter, and left it to the people to decide whether they would keep the sacred month or not.

This was the finishing stroke. From that time the Convention, as a
15 body, had only to wind up its affairs; its prestige was gone.

Ibid pp 143–4

(g) The Convention – a comment by Gammage

... at the sitting of the Convention on September the 6th, O'Brien made a motion that the body should dissolve, which was seconded

by Dr. Taylor; eleven voted for the motion and eleven against. Frost, the chairman, gave his casting vote for dissolution. . . . Such was the
5　end of the first Convention, which numbered amongst its members many men of superior talents, but who were so divided on matters of policy, as to bring about results fatal to the glorious mission which they had undertaken. The great mistake of the Convention was in presuming to act before they were possessed of the requisite power
10　to ensure success. A portion of the body was too timid and sluggish, another portion too hasty and precipitate, and those possessing the requisite energy to accelerate the cause, and preserve the even balance between the two extremes were but few, too few to turn the current of popular opinion in the right direction. A considerable
15　number were ever vacillating between the fear of danger on the one hand, and the taunts of cowardice on the other. The paucity of signature to the petition was proof that much of the work of conversion was yet to be accomplished; and if they had set themselves steadily to that work instead of trying to force ulterior
20　measures on a people as yet unprepared for their adoption, they would have produced fifty times as much good. . . . The untiring perseverance of O'Brien, and a few others, saved the country from a horrible carnage, which must inevitably have followed any attempt to carry out the sacred month. . . .

　　　R. C. Gammage, op cit, pp 156–7

(h) Persecution and prosecution

The years 1839 and '40 were years of persecution and imprisonment for the poor Chartists, our Reform Government appearing to vie with their Tory predecessors in endeavouring most cruelly to crush out the agitation for universal suffrage etc. . . . I have the names, etc.
5　of 93 Chartists who were undergoing various terms of imprison-ment at the end of 1840, including Frost, Williams and Jones, and 17 others at Monmouth, at Chester 12, including William Benbow of Middlewich, Liverpool 32, including the Rev. W. V. Jackson, Bronterre O'Brien, J. R. Richardson and Christopher Doyle . . .
10　York 23, nearly the whole of them for delivering seditious speeches.
　　　Dr. P. M. McDouall and the Rev. J. R. Stephens were tried at the Chester Assizes held in August 1839. I walked to Chester for the purpose of being present at these trials. The indictment in each case was misdemeanour, McDouall for having attended an unlawful
15　meeting held at Hyde on the 22nd of April 1839, and with having used seditious and inflammatory language. . . . On the departure of the Grand Jury, McDouall said humourously to the jury, 'Gentle-men, you may possibly have heard of Captain Scott, a celebrated American marksman. Well, once he levelled his gun at an old racoon.
20　"Hello are you Captain Scott", said the racoon, "don't fire, I'll come down and give in. You're sure to hit me." So with me, gentlemen, I

may as well give in, I'm sure to be hit.' McDouall was found guilty and sentenced to one year's imprisonment, and was bound over to keep the peace for five years, himself in £500 and two sureties of £200
25 each.

Thompson, the gunmaker, Higgins and others were tried in the same court for seditious conspiracy and sentenced to various terms of imprisonment. During these trials the barristers' table was covered with arms of various kinds, guns, swords, pikes etc, which
30 had been found in the possession of the defendants, offering on sale. This exhibition of arms in court, it was believed, was for the purpose of influencing the jury to convict. On my way to the Assizes I met on the road between Tarvin and Chester pickets of the Cheshire Yeomanry on the lookout for the expected mob from Lancashire and
35 Staffordshire coming to rescue the Chartist prisoners. . . . In addition. . . a large number of special constables were sworn in to protect and assist the authorities in the event of a rescue of the political prisoners being attempted.

> Thomas Dunning, 'Reminiscences' printed in D. Vincent, op cit, pp 136–8

Questions

a Using document (a) explain the setting up of the Convention in 1839.

b What difficulties did the Convention encounter from within the Chartist movement itself?

c What difficulties did the Convention encounter from outside Chartism?

d Why was the Convention moved to Birmingham?

e Using document (d) discuss the proposition that the views of the Birmingham authorities and the Chartists differed over the right of free speech and explain why you think this difference existed. Documents (e), (f) and (g) by Lowery and Gammage chart the Convention as an 'anti-Parliament'. Discuss.

g Documents (e), (f) and (g) by Lowery and Gammage chart the end of the Convention. Why did it fail in its objectives? Which of the two authors provides the better explanation in your view and why?

h How does document (h) show the ways in which authority reacted to Chartism?

* i The Convention placed emphasis on its constitutional position. This seriously weakened its potential as a revolutionary body. Discuss.

Further work

a Using A. Briggs (ed) Chartist Studies (London, 1959) or Gammage's work cited above or your local record office choose an area where Chartism played a role and examine how it developed between 1836 and 1840.

b Was Chartism ever viable as a national political movement?

c The Charter and the Convention emphasised human rights, but what the working class really wanted was food. Discuss.

d Using reference works such as the *Dictionary of National Biography* and the *Dictionary of Labour History* examine the lives of the leaders mentioned in this chapter. Do they have anything in common?

e How do you think Chartism could have succeeded in its objectives in its early years?

f How does the study of Chartism demonstrate the problem of generalisation for the historian?

III Chartism as Revolution: the Newport Rising and Agitation in the North

Introduction

The Newport Rising was the last rebellion in English history, yet John Frost was not a revolutionary and Newport was not a key centre. Frost was a former mayor and a magistrate, who was sentenced to death for his foolish escapade (in which 14 rebels were shot) but was transported to New South Wales instead of being hanged, drawn and quartered; he was pardoned in 1854, after which he regained respectability.

England had experienced previous disturbances in the Swing Riots of the 1830s (during which 9 men were hanged, 400 imprisoned and 400 transported) and the Reform Riots of 1831 in Bristol, but these did not match up to the revolutionary outbreaks of 1830 and 1848 in Paris, Berlin and Vienna. London was neglected because it was not the capital of industry and it did not have a large concentration of industrial workers, although an additional bastion was added to the northern outer wall of the Tower of London between 1839 and 1842.

The north was quite different, however, and industrial towns like Bolton experienced considerable disturbances during the 'Sacred Month' of 1839. These risings could have been very dangerous but for the army, under a sympathetic but firm commander, the railway and the telegraph. The army, wrote G. J. Harney, was 'seated like a spider in the centre of its web, on the diverging lines of iron road'. Why did the army stay loyal despite so much revolutionary propaganda? Ebenezer Elliott, a Sheffield poet and Chartist leader, thundered, 'What hope have you but in yourselves? Will your enemies help you? From the time of the first murderers [the rich] have been what they are!'

Social conditions, portrayed by writers as diverse as Napier, Engels and Disraeli, were a crucial factor, especially the impact of the 1834 Poor Law Amendment Act. Napier referred in December 1839 to 'the thrice-accursed new poor law, its bastiles, and its guardians. Lying title! They guard nothing, not even their own carcases. . . they so outrage misery.'

1 The National Holiday

'Depend upon it,' said Gerard, 'we must stick to the National Holiday: we can do nothing effectively, unless the movement is simultaneous. They have not troops to cope with a simultaneous movement, and the Holiday is the only machinery to secure unity of
5 action. No work for six weeks, and the rights of Labour will be acknowledged!'

'We shall never be able to make the people unanimous in a cessation of labour,' said a pale young man, very thin, but with a countenance of remarkable energy. 'The selfish instincts will come
10 into play and will balk our political object, while a great increase of physical suffering must be inevitable.'

'It might be done,' said a middle-aged thickset man, in a thoughtful tone. 'If the Unions were really to put their shoulder to the wheel, it might be done.'

15 'And if it is not done,' said Gerard, 'what do you propose? The people ask you to guide them. Shrink at such a conjuncture, and our influence over them is forfeited and justly forfeited.'

'I am for partial but extensive insurrections,' said the young man. 'Sufficient in extent and number to demand all the troops and yet to
20 distract the military movements. We can count on Birmingham again, if we act at once before their new Police Act is in force; Manchester is ripe; and several of the cotton towns; but above all I have letters that assure me that at this moment we can do anything in Wales.'

25 'Glamorganshire is right to a man,' said Wilkins, a Baptist teacher. 'And trade is so bad that the Holiday at all events must take place there, for the masters themselves are extinguishing their furnaces.'

'All the North is seething,' said Gerard.

'We must contrive to agitate the metropolis,' said Maclast, a
30 shrewd carroty-haired paper-stainer. 'We must have weekly meetings at Kennington and demonstrations at White Conduit House; we cannot do more here, I fear, than talk, but a few thousand men on Kennington Common every Saturday and some spicy resolutions will keep the Guards in London.'

35 'Aye, aye,' said Gerard; 'I wish the woollen and cotton trades were as bad to do as the iron, and we should need no holiday as you say, Wilkins. However it will come. In the meantime the Poor Law pinches and terrifies, and will make even the most spiritless turn.'

'The accounts to-day from the North are very encouraging
40 though,' said the young man. 'Stevens is producing a great effect, and this plan of our people going in procession and taking possession of the churches very much affects the imagination of the multitude.'

'Ah!' said Gerard, 'if we could only have the Church on our side, as in the good old days, we would soon put an end to the demon
45 tyranny of Capital.'

46   THE CHARTISTS

'And now,' said the pale young man, taking up a manuscript paper, 'to our immediate business. Here is the draft of the projected proclamation of the Convention on the Birmingham outbreak. It enjoins peace and order, and counsels the people to arm themselves
50 in order to secure both. You understand: that they may resist if the troops and the police endeavour to produce disturbance.'

'Aye, aye,' said Gerard. 'Let it be stout. We will settle this at once, and so get it out to-morrow. Then for action.'

'But we must circulate this pamphlet of the Polish Count on the
55 manner of encountering cavalry with pikes,' said Maclast.

''Tis printed,' said the stout thickset man; 'we have set it up on a broadside. We have sent ten thousand to the North and five thousand to John Frost. We shall have another delivery to-morrow. It takes very generally.'

60 The pale young man then read the draft of the proclamation; it was canvassed and criticized sentence by sentence; altered, approved; finally put to the vote, and unanimously carried. On the morrow it was to be posted in every thoroughfare of the metropolis, and circulated in every great city of the provinces and every populous
65 district of labour.

'And now,' said Gerard, 'I shall to-morrow to the North, where I am wanted. But before I go, I propose, as suggested yesterday, that we five, together with Langley, whom I counted on seeing here to-night, now form ourselves into a committee for arming the
70 people. Three of us are permanent in London; Wilkins and myself will aid you in the provinces. Nothing can be decided on this head till we see Langley, who will make a communication from Birmingham that cannot be trusted to writing. The seven-o'clock train must have long since arrived. He is now a good hour behind his time.'

Benjamin Disraeli, *Sybil or The Two Nations*, 1845 (1929 edn), pp 329–31

Questions

a   Explain the references to: 'the National Holiday (lines 1–2); 'We can count on Birmingham again' (lines 20–1); 'the Poor Law pinches and terrifies' (lines 37–8); 'Stevens' (line 40); 'Taking possession of the churches' (lines 41–2); 'John Frost' (line 58).

b   What is the significance of the remarks that 'they have not troops to cope with a simultaneous movement' (lines 3–4) and 'if we act at once before their new Police Act is in force' (line 21)?

c   On the basis of this document which areas and trades seemed to support Chartism and why?

d   What dilemma between moral and physical force is exposed here?

e   Comment on the impact of this passage as (i) history, and (ii) literature.

2 A Chartist Proclamation

ENGLISHMEN!

The few remaining liberties which a Tyrannical Oligarchy has left to the Enslaved People, have been this day forcibly taken from You in Birmingham by an Armed Power.

5   In vain does the British Constitution declare that every Subject has a right to petition the Queen on his Grievances. The Government, through the Magistrates, have denied that right; and have, in opposition to every principle of Justice, and of the Constitution, prevented a Meeting, called for the purpose of Peaceably Memorializing the Queen: having first brought into the Town an

10   ARMED POWER to enforce their unjustifiable and unconstitutional Proceedings.

We issue out our

SOLEMN PROTEST

against such undisguised Tyranny; declaring, that, if such an

15   encroachment on the Rights of Englishmen is submitted to, there will be no longer Freedom for any class. Tyranny preserving its power only by abridging the Liberties of all.

We record it as our deliberate opinion, that the Ruling Power has taken away the just and Constitutional Rights of the People, and that

20   circumstances have now arisen, in which the Government has no rightful claim to our allegiance.

PASSIVE RESISTANCE on our part is not only a Right but a SACRED DUTY.

We Resolve

NOT TO OBEY THE GOVERNMENT

25   By Serving Them in any Capacity

WE RESOLVE NOT TO RECOGNIZE THEM AS OUR GOVERNMENT;
We, therefore, REFUSE

TO PAY ALL TAXES.

30   Signed, by order of the Committee,
Christian Chartist Church.   Arthur o'Neill, Secretary.

Trueman, Printer, Chartist Press, Newhall–street, Birmingham.
Lambeth Palace Library, quoted in J. Addy and E. G. Power (eds), *The Industrial Revolution*, 1976, p 131

Questions

a   What was the background in Birmingham to this document?

b   Examine and comment on the emotive words and phrases used in this handbill, for example, 'tyrannical oligarchy' (line 1).

c   What did the Chartists hope to achieve by refusing to pay taxes? Why may this group not have urged stronger action?

d   Do lines 24–9 illustrate the lack of realism shown by many Chartists?

3   John Frost, J.P.

Newport, Monmouthshire, 19 Jan. 1839

My Lord – In your lordship's letter of the 16th there is a mistake. I am
not a magistrate for the county of Monmouth, but for the borough
of Newport. . . .

5   In the spring of 1835, the council of the borough recommended me
as a proper person to be a justice of the peace. I was appointed, and I
believe that the inhabitants will bear honourable testimony as to the
manner in which I have performed the duties of that office. . . .
For what does your lordship think it incumbent to get my name

10   erased from the commission of the peace? For attending a meeting at
Pontypool on the 1st of January? . . . I deny that violent and
inflammatory language was used. . . . There was a time when the
Whig Ministry was not so fastidious as to violent and inflammatory
language uttered at public meetings. . . .

15   It appears from the letter of your lordship that I, if present at a public
meeting, should be answerable for language uttered by others. If
these are to be the terms on which Her Majesty's commission of the
peace is to be holden, take it back again, for surely none but the most
servile of men would hold it on such terms. . . .

20   Is it an offence to be appointed a delegate to convey to the constituted
authorities the petitions of the people? . . . I know of no body calling
itself a convention. Your lordship is aware that a convention existed
at one time in this country. Your lordship is aware what this
convention did, and that its acts are called glorious. . . .

25   Twenty years' reading and experience have convinced me that the
only method to produce and secure that state of things, is a
restoration of the ancient constitution. Deeply impressed with this
conviction, I have laboured to obtain the end by means recognized
by the laws of my country – petition; and for this your lordship

30   thinks I ought to be stricken off the commission of the peace! . . . I am
convinced that in my own neighbourhood my attending public
meetings has tended to restrain violent language. Does your lordship
wish that the peace should be preserved? I have always been a
preserver of the peace, and of this your lordship may be convinced

35   by applying to the duke of Beaufort and Lord Granville Somerset.
Probably your lordship is unaccustomed to language of this
description; that, my lord, is a misfortune. Much of the evils of life
proceeds from the want of sincerity in those who hold converse with
men in authority. Simple men like those best, who prophesy smooth

40   things.

I remain yours,
JOHN FROST.

John Frost to Lord John Russell, *Annual Register*, 1839
(Chronicle), pp 22–6, quoted in D. Williams, *John Frost*, 1939,
pp 124–6

Questions

a What had happened to make Frost write this letter to the Home Secretary?

b What arguments did Frost use to plead his case?

c Explain the references to 'the Whig Ministry' (lines 12–13) and 'a convention' (line 22).

d What image of Frost emerges from this letter? How does it compare with his subsequent actions?

4 Newport

Edward Patton, a carpenter of Newport, deposed as follows: The parcel of people I saw in the morning of the riot, were armed; they had guns, sticks, etc.; the sticks had iron points, I did not see many with guns. I saw of this body two hundred or three hundred. There
5 were not many more. I had full view of those on Stowe Hill. I was a little bit alarmed, but not particularly so, but I wished to see what they would say and do. I was not at work that morning. I did not hear that they were to come down from the hills. I believe that a great number of them went to the gates from the hotel. I know the two
10 bow-windows in front of the Westgate. I never saw anything done to the windows of the Westgate. I did not hear a crash of the windows. They were not very tumultuous. They drew up in front of the Westgate. I am certain they said that the prisoners were taken before daylight. It was about nine o'clock in the morning when they came
15 down Stowe Hill. It was broad daylight two hours before that. Those that were in the Westgate were taken before daylight. The body of the mob stood for a space, and asked for the prisoners who were taken before daylight. None of the mob went forward as spokesmen. They came close to the door. I could only see the steps, to which the
20 mob came close up. The first moment or two they asked for the prisoner Smith; then a rush was made. Then I heard firing, and took to my heels. I cannot say whether the mob had guns, pikes or clubs. I cannot tell whether they were armed for the biggest part. I heard some one say, in a very loud voice, 'No, never.' I was distant from
25 the door of the Westgate twenty-five yards when I heard the words. I heard no groaning. I could not say where the firing began. No man could judge. You nor I could not tell. Saw no smoke outside. It is likely enough the firing began from the Westgate Inn. . . .

> *Annual Register*, 1840, pp 215–16, quoted in E. Royle, *Chartism*, 1980, pp 96–7

At least eight thousand men, mostly miners employed in the
30 neighbourhood (which is very densely populated) were engaged in the attack upon the town of Newport and . . . many of them were armed. Their design seems to have been to wreak their vengeance

upon the Newport magistrates, for the prosecution of Vincent and
others, now lying in Monmouth gaol, and after securing the town, to
35 advance to Monmouth and liberate these prisoners. The ultimate
design of the leaders does not appear; but it probably was to rear the
standard of rebellion throughout Wales, in hopes of being able to
hold the royal forces at bay, in that mountainous district, until the
people of England, assured by successes, should rise, *en masse*, for the
40 same objects. . . . Mr. Frost, the late member of the Convention led
the rioters, and he, with others, has been committed for high treason.
On entering Newport, the people marched straight to the Westgate
Hotel, where the magistrates, with about 40 soldiers were assembled, being fully apprised of the intended outbreak. The Riot Act was
45 read, and the soldiers fired down, with ease and security, upon the
people who had first broken and fired into the windows. The people
in a few minutes found their position untenable, and retired to the
outside of the town, to concert a different plan of attack, but
ultimately returned home, without attempting anything more. The
50 soldiers did not leave their place of shelter to follow them. About
thirty of the people are known to have been killed, and several to
have been wounded. . . . It is fortunate that the people did not think
of setting fire to the buildings adjoining the Westgate Hotel, which
would have compelled the soldiers to quit their stronghold, and
55 surrender themselves . . . but it is far better for the sacred cause of
liberty that this foolish rising was so ill-conducted as to be checked at
the outset. The rioters did not disgrace themselves by any wanton
destruction of property nor by plunder. The Chartists, as a body, are
too well-informed to offer any countenance or encouragement to
60 any such resorts to violence, for the attainment of their just rights.

'Reformator', *Charter*, 17 November 1839, quoted in P.
Hollis (ed), *Class and Conflict in Nineteenth Century England
1815–1850*, 1973, pp 243–4

Questions

a   On the basis of these two reports, (i) what was the aim of Frost
and his associates, and (ii) what actually happened?
b   Is there any evidence that the rising was expected?
c   At what point in his deposition did Patton change his description
of the people involved in the attack?
d   Which of the two accounts is less sympathetic to the rising? What
might account for this?
e   'A rising' or 'a mass demonstration'. Which of these definitions
best fits this event?

5 Counter-intelligence

My Dear Mary Anne

You are the prince of correspondents but I do not wish you to do so again unless you think it of importance and above all do not ever
5   put your initials but take another name altogether, as the name of the Town is sufficient. . . . Matters are coming to a crisis and that in short space, *Frost shall not be tried,* or will have companions he little thinks of, keep this in mind and be astonished at nothing, depend upon it there will be a merry Christmas, all here are already
10   preparing for a national Illumination, I presume in anticipation of the Queens Marriage, but you know best: – these Radicals are terrible fellows, at least half a dozen Emissaries have been sent to see what state the North of England was in and the universal feeling is that there is no county like xxxx this is partly to be attributed to the vast
15   extent of Moorland which has generated a race of hardy Poachers all well armed, and who would think themselves disgraced if they missed a moorcock flying seventy yards off, this together with the number of Weavers necessarily in want has made a population ripe for action and its neighbourhood to the Scotish Border with the
20   facilities for a guerilla warfare are said to have determined xxxx to make it the Head quarters for a winter campaign – that he is mad enough to attempt this you will easily believe even if there were no other movement in England because from the feeling of the people towards him they would follow him to the death, and England has
25   not Troops enough to quell a Border riot with that man at its head: it is too far away however to have any effect for a long time.

It is said your Irish friend O'Connor has proved himself the Coward his Enemies always called him and having before betrayed the men of England in the matter of the strikes has now refused to
30   take part with the men of his own county (Yorkshire) – he is agitating for money to pay Lawyers, as if money could save Frost when he knows that every Lawyer would give ten years Briefs to hang him, if it is to be done at all, other means must be used and the Chartists are not worth the name of men if they dont try them. . . .
35   It is commonly reported that the Radicals are gathering in great strength in Wales, and that nothing prevents their rising in the Heart of England, but the want of a Leader who would have the confidence of all, they applied in vain to the Boasters and finding them cowards determined to do the work themselves and sent to a *friend* of yours to
40   know whether if they did so he would make a diversion in their favour, his answer was characteristic viz. that if they would give him five Regiments each of 800 armed and determined men he would lead them himself, as he thought a blow in the Heart of England and which involved the possession of many Towns and their destruction

45 upon the first attempt to arrest them back again would be more
effectual than any other. . . .
    I need not tell you to remember me kindly to all old friends and for
obvious reasons I do not mention them. I care little for ——s
preaching but I think if he is honest he might be better employed in
50 shewing his loyalty by preparing an universal Illumination in
Birmingham. I have now resolved to trust no one with my plans
because if I survive I can carry them out alone. . . .
    Once more Farewell to you and all old friends, if we meet again it
will be in Freedom and in peace. In the present crisis I do not think any
55 Bank in England will stand.

Lt. Colonel Pringle Taylor to the Mayor of Southampton

Sunday 11th January 1840
    . . . A most influential Chartist Delegate from the North, who was
all for physical force and violent measures, was led by one of our men
through Birmingham and London to prove to him that all that
60 organization which existed previously in these towns was quite
destroyed the effects produced upon him and through him upon the
other Delegates by the unexpected change in these places – the result
of our action led to such representations to the various leaders that
their minds were paralysed and the intended general outbreak on
65 New Years Eve was postponed but to what period I have not yet
learned – a spark would ignite the combustible materials and bring
upon us all the horrors of a servile [?civil] war. . . .

Lt. Colonel Pringle Taylor to the Marquis of Normanby

20th January 1840
    . . . I also mentioned him by name to Colonel Yorke as having
70 been elected the Delegate of the Chartists of Spitalfields, I believed
the only remaining London District organized for outbreak, the
organization of which this foreigner was the origin having been as I
was informed and as I formerly represented to your Lordship the
means of combining a million and a half or two millions of the adult
75 labouring male population throughout the whole kingdom, for
simultaneous nocturnal outbreaks every where aggressive, with the
lighted torch and murderous arm, but never to resist still less to assail
the military Force. . . .

Lt. Colonel Pringle Taylor to the Marquis of Anglesey

27th January 1840
80 My Lord
    The general expectation which seems suddenly to have arisen that
the extreme penalty of the Law will be made to fall on Mr Frost and
his accomplices, induces me to address your Lordship under a feeling

of deep responsibility, arising from the reflection, that if Her Majesty
85 were apprized of all that has taken place, in regard to the communication which your Lordship made to Lord Normanby, a month before
the Newport outbreak, Her Majesty might be induced to exercise
the Prerogative of Mercy in favour of the misguided men under
sentence of Death.
90   As regards myself and the Gentlemen associated with me in the
object of paralyzing the destructive character of Chartism, we have
been alone actuated, from the first moment of our acquiring a
knowledge of its alarming organization and revolutionary objects,
by feelings of loyalty as Citizens, and of our duty as men, to prevent
95 crime and bloodshed. We have studiously abstained from mixing up
this affair with any objects of party, having had no desire to implicate
the Government, either for its ignorance of the internal state of
England during so long a period, or for its subsequent neglect of the
communication on this subject made by me through your Lordship.
100 I cannot however but confess my alarm at the position in which the
Government and the country may possibly be placed, if, through the
event of Mr Frost's execution, the sympathy of the Chartists were to
be re-excited, and to be reacted upon, by the community at large
coming to the knowledge, that means might have been adopted by
105 the Government to anticipate the calamitous events in Wales, and
my anxiety is greatly increased on reflecting that as the whole of our
exertions have been carried on openly and without any disguise, we
possess no means of preventing their becoming more publicly
known. . . .

> Lt. Col. Pringle Taylor, *Letters Relative to the Chartists* . . . ,
> 1839–40, pp 15–18, 22, 24, 29, 31–4 (Bodleian Library,
> Oxford 2288 c. 53)

Questions

a Who is supposed to have written the first letter, and what
   significant information did it contain?

b Which county is probably referred to in line 14?

c How realistic and reliable do you think this correspondent was?

d What message was Pringle Taylor trying to convey in the letter
   to the Mayor of Southampton?

e Comment on the arguments used in the fourth letter against
   Frost's execution.

f Distinguish in these letters between evidence and hypothesis.
   Which points need further checking, and what kind of sources
   could be used?

g Which of the following seems to approximate most closely to
   Pringle Taylor's role:
   (i) an army officer carrying out his normal duties;
   (ii) an *agent provocateur*;

(iii) an undercover agent;
(iv) an army officer employed on Intelligence duties?
How does your choice affect an understanding of the events of
1839?

6   Industrial Lancashire

In Lancashire, and especially in Manchester, English manufacture
finds at once its starting-point and its centre. . . . In the cotton
industry of South Lancashire, the application of the forces of Nature,
the superseding of hand-labour by machinery (especially by the
5   power-loom and the self-acting mule), and the division of labour, are
seen at the highest point; and, if we recognize in these three elements
that which is characteristic of modern manufacture, we must confess
that the cotton industry has remained in advance of all other
branches of industry from the beginning down to the present day.
10   The effects of modern manufacture upon the working-class must
necessarily develop here most freely and perfectly, and the manufacturing proletariat present itself in its fullest classic perfection. The
degradation to which the application of steam-power, machinery
and the division of labour reduce the working-man, and the attempts
15   of the proletariat to rise above this abasement, must likewise be
carried to the highest point and with the fullest consciousness. . . .
The towns surrounding Manchester vary little from the central
city, so far as the working-people's quarters are concerned, except
that the working-class forms, if possible, a larger proportion of their
20   population. These towns are purely industrial and conduct all their
business through Manchester upon which they are in every respect
dependent, whence they are inhabited only by working-men and
petty tradesmen, while Manchester has a very considerable commercial population, especially of commission and 'respectable' retail
25   dealers. Hence Bolton, Preston, Wigan, Bury, Rochdale, Middle-
ton, Heywood, Oldham, Ashton, Stalybridge, Stockport, etc.,
though nearly all towns of thirty, fifty, seventy to ninety thousand
inhabitants, are almost wholly working-people's districts, inter-
spersed only with factories, a few thoroughfares lined with shops, and
30   a few lanes along which the gardens and houses of the manufacturers
are scattered like villas. The towns themselves are badly and
irregularly built with foul courts, lanes, and back alleys, reeking of
coal smoke, and especially dingy from the originally bright red
brick, turned black with time, which is here the universal building
35   material. Cellar dwellings are general here; wherever it is in any way
possible, these subterranean dens are constructed, and a very
considerable portion of the population dwells in them.
Among the worst of these towns after Preston and Oldham is
Bolton, eleven miles north-west of Manchester. It has, so far as I
40   have been able to observe in my repeated visits, but one main street, a

very dirty one, Deansgate, which serves as a market, and is even in the finest weather a dark, unattractive hole in spite of the fact that, except for the factories, its sides are formed by low one- and two-storied houses. Here, as everywhere, the old part of the town is especially ruinous and miserable. A dark-coloured body of water, which leaves the beholder in doubt whether it is a brook or a long string of stagnant puddles, flows through the town, and contributes its share to the total pollution of the air, by no means pure without it. . . .

> Frederick Engels, *The Condition of the Working-Class in England*, 1892 (1969 edn), pp 75–6

Questions

a Why did Engels consider that 'the effects of modern manufacture upon the working-class must necessarily develop here most freely and perfectly' (lines 10–11)?

b How did the towns around Manchester differ from the great 'cottonopolis'? How might this have affected their inclination to Chartism?

c What effect might social and economic conditions have had on the growth of Chartism in Bolton?

d How had Engels obtained his information, and what part did he play in nineteenth-century politics and society?

e Investigate Chartist activities in Manchester and adjacent towns, and comment on the validity of Christopher Thorne's statement that 'the greatest immediate cause of Chartism as a mass movement was economic hardship'.

7   Bolton: a Micro-study

(a) THE BOLTON CHARTISTS – On Sunday morning last at an early hour, the chartists mustered on the New Market Place, for the purpose of again proceeding to the parish church. The morning being exceedingly fine, great crowds of persons were attracted into the principal streets to witness the proceedings. The chartists seemed rather disconcerted towards ten o'clock, as their numbers by no means answered their anticipations. After the bells had commenced ringing, however, they formed themselves; and, on moving off the square, their numbers, on being counted, were found to be little more than six hundred, a large proportion of them being boys. On arriving at the church, they found the police and others busily engaged in making way for them through the crowd, and inviting them forward; but, on entering the church, they were somewhat disappointed in finding it about half filled with the usual members of the congregation. They were, therefore, obliged to procure seats where they could. Their conduct during the service was unusually

decorous, probably owing to the sprinkling of other parties amongst them. The Rev. Mr. Robin, the curate, delivered an impressive sermon, though not particularly appropriate to the occasion. At the
20 close of the service, they returned to the New Market Place; and, in the afternoon, a local preacher from Bury, of their own creed in politics, delivered a short sermon. In the evening Richard Carlile delivered a lecture, exposing some of their follies, but recommending them to continue their attendance at the church, which he said
25 belonged to the people; and, if they were not satisfied with the minister provided for them, to elect one of their own, and place him in a pulpit in the church. He then proceeded to read over the 6th chapter of Timothy, and grounded his text on the same verse as that selected by the curate on last Sunday but one, and at the conclusion of
30 his harangue appealed to them as to which had made the best sermon; as much as to say, 'If the clergyman does not suit you, appoint me in his stead.' The day passed off without the slightest disturbance, although many persons were in great fear that such extraordinary proceedings were calculated to end in nothing but a
35 desecration of the Sabbath.

The *Manchester Guardian*, 7 August 1839

(b)   Saturday August 17 1839

On Sunday the Chartists marched to church . . . the greater portion having betaken them to other places of more easy and grateful resort. Great apprehension was expressed by the inhabitants of the town that violence would be attempted. At the latter part of last week,
5 therefore, about 1500 special constables were sworn in, and other arrangements made to preserve the peace of the town. It is not for us as reporters, to express our opinion regarding the origin of such meetings, nor do we wish to express our own sentiments regarding the proper persons who should have been made responsible for the
10 consequences. Whether incited by the Mayor or his friends it is not for us to consider, whether the property of the town was placed in jeopardy by the men who had for years fostered the notions entertained by the Chartists it is not for us to determine. . . . The industrious operatives in the town took no share in the disturbances.
15 A number of irritated ill-advised young men were the principal actors. . . .

MONDAY–. . . . The town was in a state of the greatest alarm; the major part of the shops in the Market-place were closed. To have witnessed the state of public feeling throughout the morning, one
20 would have considered a terrible attack to be at hand. . . . No arms of any kind were displayed by the Chartists, but sufficient was indicated to manifest the animus of the assembly. . . .

TUESDAY–. . . . at five o'clock [a.m.] the Chartists again assembled . . . numbering . . . about 300. The police officers with the warrant

25   against the leaders . . . made no effort to disperse the mob when first
      collecting. . . . [Later the leaders, including a Chartist delegate, were
      arrested, and the crowd attempted to rescue them] showers of stones
      were thrown in all directions, the vociferations were prodigious . . .
      the commotion . . . arrived at a tremendous pitch. The mayor and
30   magistrates consulted and . . . determined upon reading the riot act.
      The military, comprising two companies of the 96th Foot . . . was
      instantly called out, and were promptly on the spot. . . . The
      appearance of the military as a defensive or if necessary offensive
      body discouraged the multitude. . . .

      The *Bolton Chronicle*, 17 August 1839

(c) Our readers are no doubt aware that considerable mystery hangs
over certain circumstances connected with the riot at the Town Hall,
Little Bolton, on the 13th ult. According to Lord Lyndhurst . . . the
rioters were informed by the Mayor that they might burn down the
5   Town Hall if they pleased. According to common rumour in Bolton,
Mr. John Fletcher could have put an end to the riot long before there
was any serious damage done, and yet delayed doing so for two
hours. . . .
Lord Lyndhurst stated that the account brought to the Police Office
10   were, that the mob had commenced pulling down the Town Hall;
but then his object was to blacken the Mayor's character. Mr.
Fletcher says, 'Reports were brought that in Little Bolton the mob
was ill-treating the special constables.' This is rather mild language
to use about a riot such as was then taking place at the Town Hall; for
15   . . . this is said to have been 'about seven o'clock,' at which time the
special constables had been held in *durance vile* by the mob nearly an
hour. Our information . . . was, that Mr. John Fletcher was actually
present, when one or more persons deposed that the special
constables were then besieged in the Town Hall by an infuriated
20   mob, and we naturally concluded that, if he did hear such a
deposition, it was his duty to order out the military immediately,
even on his own responsibility. But it appears that his impression
was that the affair in Little Bolton, did not at that time require the
presence of the military. If so, he must have seen with much pain the
25   malignant and false charges brought against the Mayor, by the
Chronicle and other Tory journals, for neglecting to call out the
military.

      The *Bolton Free Press*, 7 September 1839

(d) [1839]
April 9th The troops are in twenty-six detachments, spread over
half England, some two hundred miles from me! The magistrates are
divided into Whigs, Tories, and personal enmities. . . . The town
magistrates are liberal from fear of the populace; the country bucks
5   are too old and too far gone Tories to have hopes of gaining

popularity by being Radical; so they labour to get troops near their own houses. *Funk* is the order of the day, and there is some excuse, for the people seem ferocious enough. But this fear has produced a foolish dispersion of the troops, these magistrates being powerful
10 fellows. . . .
April 23rd These poor people are inclined to rise, and if they do what horrid bloodshed! This is dreadful work, would to God I had gone to Australia. . . .
August 15th Napoleon's birthday! All quiet. The magistrates
15 wanted me to call out the yeomanry. No said I no yeomen. If the Chartists want a fight, they can be indulged without yeomen, who are over-zealous for cutting and slashing. . . .
August 17th Bolton is the only place where shot has been fired, but only three there, and those from the eagerness of the magistrates. . . .
20 August 20th . . . The mayor and corporation of Bolton are said to be Chartists . . . the constables everywhere are, more or less, and all avow that the people are oppressed.
December 1st Poor creatures, their threats of attack are miserable. With half a cartridge, and half a pike, with no money, no discipline,
25 no skilful leaders, they would attack men with leaders, money and discipline, well armed, and having sixty rounds a man. Poor men!
[n.d.] Every element of a ferocious civil war is boiling in this district . . . of all classes the worst are the magistrates. The Tory magistrates are bold, violent, irritating, and uncompromising; the Whig magis-
30 trates sneaking and base, always ready to call for troops, and yet truckling to the mob. . . .

> Sir W. Napier, *Life and Opinions of General Sir Charles Napier*,
> 1857, II, pp 7–8, 12, 72–5, 93, 153

(e) [John Warden and George Lloyd of Bolton, defendants at the Liverpool Assizes, April 1840] Attorney General, in opening this case, said this was a prosecution of a serious character. The 12th of August last. . . was the day intended for the National Holiday. . . . In
5 the town of Bolton on that occasion mobs of people assembled of an alarming character, a stop was put to all public confidence and security, and public business was suspended; the military had to be called in; and the Riot Act had to be read. The indictment charged the two defendants with being concerned in that riot. . . .
10   Frederick M. Baker called – Witness said he was a police officer at Bolton. . . . A great number of people assembled during the day; and the effect was that the shopkeepers closed their shops, and business was almost entirely suspended. . . . On the morning of the 12th, he saw Lloyd about six o'clock addressing the mob. . . . He heard him
15 say they were not to cause disturbance, but if interfered with, to act like men determined to have their rights. Let their tyrants see they were not to be frightened into surrender of their birthright, but that they were determined to have it, and willing to die for the cause.

They dispersed after that, and assembled again in the Market-
20 place. . . . Lloyd then addressed them, and said he was not an advocate
for rioting, but he would have them remember that the Reform Bill
was gained by the riots at Bristol. – The mob continued to meet
during the day. In the evening many thousands assembled again, and
it was such a multitude that the civil force could not contend
25 with. . . . They then paraded the streets, some of them carrying
bludgeons. There was great shouting, hooting the police, and
creating great terror in the people. Even the shutters of private
houses were closed. Witness, after the proceedings of the 12th
received directions to apprehend the prisoners. . . .
30 A police officer named Bradshaw was next called, and stated that
the crowd on the 12th of August went about to a number of factories
and induced the workmen to leave their work. . . . The defendants
were leaders of the crowd. Would give instances. They fell in rank
when Lloyd told them, and *they insisted on rescuing him when he told*
35 *them to be quiet.* (A laugh).

John Nicholson. Tea-dealer, Hotel-street, Bolton, was a special
constable on the 12th August. At seven o'clock in the morning of
that day, he saw a crowd there of 500 or more. He heard Lloyd say,
the time is now arrived when the Charter must either become the
40 law of the land, or we must remain passive slaves in the hands of our
enemies. Be firm, be resolute, and the victory is yours. Peaceable if
we can, but forcibly if we must. He then advised the crowd to take a
walk round the town with him before breakfast. They did so. . . .
The *Northern Star*, 11 April 1840, quoted in Hollis, op cit, pp
236–7

Questions

a What seems to have happened in Bolton in mid–August 1839 on
the basis of the evidence presented here?
b Discuss the point of view of each document, and assess its value.
c What criticisms were made of the Bolton magistrates and how
would you, as a magistrate, reply to your critics?
d What was General Napier's role in 1839 and why was his
response to Chartism comparatively sensible and successful?
e How does this micro–study illuminate aspects of both moral and
physical force in Chartism, as studied in this section and the
following one?
f Construct a role–play in which decisions relating to these events
in Bolton are discussed by students representing the main
protagonists.

IV   Leaders and Beliefs: Moral and Physical Force

Introduction

The main arguments between moral and physical force in Chartism have been well rehearsed by historians, yet the dichotomy was by no means a novel feature of English politics, witness the contemporary debates over the execution of King Charles I in 1649 and the abdication or desertion of his son King James II in 1688. Nor was there a simple distinction: the Sheffield Chartist Thomas Briggs said 'with respect to those gentlemen who [spoke] so much and loudly about guns and pikes and muskets . . . the best thing [for them was] to take a spade and fall out with some common', yet he later urged violent methods. As William Lovett commented, 'Muskets are not what are wanted, but education and schooling of the working people. . . . Violent words do not slay the enemies but the friends of our movement.'

If the movement's methods and even aims were varied, so were its leaders: Lovett, 'The indispensable organizer'; O'Connor, a futile idealist or a man of the people speaking in Manchester in 1842 in a fustian suit, remaining in the public eye despite the attacks levelled at him; O'Brien, the romantic, who proposed the 'Sacred Month' and saw Chartism as a social as well as political movement; Harney, an excellent writer who anticipated Marx on the class struggle and looked to Chartism as the political expression of the working class. There were also local leaders like the Revd J. R. Stephens, a Methodist preacher, who addressed 20,000 on Kersall Moor, Manchester: 'Chartism, my friends, is no political movement, where the main point is your getting the ballot. Chartism is a knife and fork question: the Charter means a good house, good food and drink, prosperity, and short working hours.'

The movement was well served by its newspapers, as shown by the *Chartist Circular* in Scotland, which sold 22,000 a week in its first year, and the *Northern Star*, the latter described by Engels as 'the only sheet which reports all the movements of the proletariat'. These newspapers compare favourably with today's tabloids in their reading level, as do the ephemeral pamphlets, often privately published and circulated.

This section concludes with Carlyle's brilliant commentary on the

'Condition of England' question – a valuable text for debates on the nineteenth century.

1 O'Connor: the Great I AM

Sir, you might have beaten the big drum of your own vanity till you grew sick of its music, and revelled in your own selfish idolatry till common sense taught your audience that the sacrifice was greater than the benefit, had you been pleased to excuse us from worship-
5 ping at your altar. But no, your own vain self must be supreme – you must be 'the leader of the people' – and from the first moment that we resolved to form an association of working men, and called upon them to manage their own affairs, *and dispense with leadership of every description*, we have had *you* and *patriots of your feelings* continually in
10 arms against us. You have made three or four attempts to get up associations in London where you might be 'the leader' – not brooking that working men should dare presume *to think of principles* instead of public idols. You have failed in all your attempts. You have christened public meetings 'great associations' to suit your purposes
15 – you have dubbed yourself 'the missionary of all the Radicals of London', your constituents being your own presumptuous boast-ings. You 'are the founder of Radical Associations!' Heaven save our ignorance! or blot out the memory of Cartwright, Hunt and Cobbett. You tell the country that you alone 'have organised the
20 Radicals of London' – and tell the Londoners the wonders your genius has performed in the country. You carry your fame about with you on all occasions to sink all other topics in the shade – you are the great 'I AM' of politics, the great personification of Radicalism – Fergus O'Connor. . . .
25 O'Connor published a shuffling reply to this in the *Northern Star*, which concluded with a threat, that 'we must either crush him, or he would annihilate our association;' a threat which evinced the spirit of the man, who, after he had made a false charge, threatened us with annihilation for complaining. . . . When I was cooped up in Warwick
30 Gaol he [O'Connor] had the impudence to boast that he was the man that prevented the Sacred Month from taking place! although . . . he was an active party in recommending it. He subsequently on several occasions endeavoured to persuade his dupes that I was the concoctor of the violent measure, although himself and his disciples
35 were the first to talk of arming, of the run upon the banks, and the Attwood project of *the sacred month*. . . .
The most serious of all the events that happened during our imprisonment was the Newport outbreak. . . . [Frost was informed that] if the Welsh effect a rising in favour of Vincent, the people of
40 Yorkshire and Lancashire . . . were ready to join in a rising for the Charter. . . . In anticipation of this rising in the North a person was

delegated from one of the towns to go to Fergus O'Connor, to request that he would lead them on, as he had so often declared he would. . . . *Delegate.* – Mr. O'Connor, we are going to have a rising
45 for the Charter, in Yorkshire, and I am sent from —— to ask if you will lead us on, as you have often said you would when we were prepared. *Fergus.* – Well, when is this rising to take place? *Delegate.* – Why, we have resolved that it shall begin on Saturday next. *Fergus.* – Are you all well provided with arms, then? *Delegate.* – Yes, all of us.
50 *Fergus.* – Well, that is all right, my man. *Delegate.* – Now, Mr. O'Connor, shall I tell our lads that you will come and lead them on? *Fergus* now indignantly replied, 'Why, man! when did you ever hear of me, or any one of my family, ever deserting the cause of the people? Have they not always been found at their post in the hour of
55 danger?' In this bouncing manner did Fergus induce the poor fellow to believe that he was ready to head the people; and he went back and made his report accordingly. But the man subsequently lost caste among his fellow-townsmen, for bringing them a false report – Fergus having solemnly assured them that he never promised him
60 anything. No sooner, however, did he find out that they were so far in earnest as described, that he set out to render the outbreak ineffectual; notwithstanding all his previous incitements to arming and preparedness, and all his boast and swaggering at public meetings, and in the columns of the 'Star,' he is said to have engaged
65 George White to go into Yorkshire and Lancashire, to assure the people that no rising would take place in Wales; and Charles Jones he sent into Wales, to assure the Welsh that there would be no rising in Yorkshire, and that it was all a government plot. . . . Fergus . . . apprehensive of being called upon to set an heroic example, in those
70 rising times, thought it a timely opportunity for visiting Ireland, so that by the time he came back most of the foolish outbreaks were over. . . .
I regard Fergus O'Connor as the chief marplot of our movement . . . a man who, by his personal conduct joined to his malignant
75 influence in the *Northern Star*, has been the blight of democracy from the first moment he opened his mouth as its *professed advocate.* . . . Not possessing a nature to appreciate intellectual exertions, he began his career by ridiculing our '*moral force humbuggery!*' . . . By his great professions, by trickery and deceit, he got the aid of the working
80 classes to establish an organ to promulgate their principles, which he soon converted into an instrument for destroying everything intellectual and moral in our movement. . . the *Star*, a mere reflex of the nature of its master. . . . By his constant appeals to the selfishness, vanity, and mere animal propensities of man, he succeeded in calling
85 up a spirit of hate, intolerance and brute feeling, previously unknown among Reformers. . . . For myself, I will have nothing to do with such a man . . . not only believing him to have done irreparable mischief to our cause, but knowing him to be politically

90 and morally dishonest; I believe he will still further injure every
cause he may be connected with. . . .
W. Lovett, *The Life and Struggles of William Lovett*, 1876, pp
161–2, 208, 238–41, 294–7

Questions

a What criticisms did Lovett make of O'Connor?
b Where was O'Connor at the time of the Newport Rising, and
why was this significant?
c Compare the account by Lovett of the 1839 Rising with those in
the previous section.
d Examine Lovett's claim that O'Connor 'will still further injure
every cause he may be connected with' (lines 89–90).
e How much significance should be attached to vituperative
attacks by rival leaders? Did these quarrels contribute to the
decline of Chartism?

2   A Chartist on Chartists

Upwards of six feet in height, stout and athletic, and in spite of his
opinions invested with a sort of aristocratic bearing, the sight of his
person was calculated to inspire the masses with a solemn awe. . . .
O'Connor's short neck . . . was the only defect in his physical
5   appearance, and even this, so far from conveying an unfavourable
impression, rather enhanced than detracted from the idea which the
public entertained of the great strength of his iron frame. . . .
His broad massive forehead . . . bore evidence . . . of great
intellectual force. To assert that he possessed a mind solid and steady
10   were to say too much, no man with an equal amount of intellect was
ever more erratic. Had the solidity of his judgment been equal to his
quickness of perception he would intellectually have been a great
man, but this essential quality of greatness he lacked, hence his life
presents a series of mistakes and contradictions. . . . No man in the
15   movement was so certain of popularity as O'Connor. No man was
so certain to lose it after its attainment. It was not till he proceeded to
speak that the full extent of his influence was felt. . . . Out of doors
O'Connor was the almost universal idol, for the thunder of his voice
would reach the ears of the most careless, and put to silence the most
20   noisy of his audience. . . . The effect was irresistible. . . .

There was one man who wielded more of the real democratic mind
than any other man in the movement; and who, with the single
exception of O'Connor, was also more generally popular. Yet this
man had been but little accustomed to the labours and honours of the
25   platform. It was through the medium of the press that his influence
had been principally felt. The name of the gentlemen . . . was James

Bronterre O'Brien. . . . There was no man more fascinating. . . . In stature he was considerably above the middle size, of fine figure, though rather inclined to the stooping posture of the profound
30   student. His general features were often adjudged to be handsome. . . . His lofty, broad, and massive brow, showed him to be a man of extraordinary mental ability. . . . He was undoubtedly the man with the greatest breadth of mind. In the Chartist ranks he was universally known as the schoolmaster, a title bestowed on him by
35   O'Connor. His veriest foes bore testimony to the greatness of his intellect. . . .

When reasoning a point he was deliberate to admiration. No other speaker was capable of rising to such a height, or of so impressing an audience with the strength and intensity of his feelings, while no
40   orator could outrival him in action and flexibility of voice. In handling the weapon of satire, he enjoyed an immeasurable superiority over all his compeers. There was no flippancy in his wit. It was grand and solid. . . . No man could so easily mould reason, satire, or declamation into one compact body, or hurl the triple weapon at the
45   head of an antagonist with more terrible force. He always enjoyed, too, the happy facility of adapting himself to the comprehension of his audience. . . . Three hours was about the usual time he occupied a meeting; but he sometimes spoke for four, and even five hours, rivetting the attention of his audience to the close of his address. . . .
50   A man who was possessed of such capabilities, was an orator of no ordinary power, and . . . he must have been a master, not only of words, but of ideas. . . .

He had but little sympathy with the class of landlords whom he looked upon as the hereditary enemies of society. But there was
55   another class whom he regarded with greater dread, viz., the great monied class, which had risen to immense importance, and whose power was on the increase. He saw in that class a multitude of persons who were living on fixed incomes. The natural tendency of Free Trade, the economists themselves admitted, would be to
60   cheapen commodities, and O'Brien argued that this would enable the usurer, the tax eater, the parson, and all other classes whose incomes were fixed, to command, with the same amount of money, an increase of those commodities, just in proportion to their cheapness, and in that proportion their incomes would thus be
65   virtually raised. He contended then, that if those parties . . . were thus enabled to command a larger share of wealth, they could obtain it only at the expense of others, those others being the labouring class, who are the source of all the wealth produced. O'Brien also took into account the state of the private debtor and creditor interests,
70   showing that debts had been contracted under the restrictive system while prices were high, and money consequently low in value, which would have to be paid under the free trade system, when prices should become low, and the value of money would conse-

quently be enhanced. . . . Since the enactment of Sir Robert Peel's
75 measures in 1846, O'Brien's views may have appeared to many to be
falsified. . . .

Gammage, op cit, pp 45, 71, 76–7, 103–4

Questions

a What did Gammage think were O'Connor's strengths and
weaknesses?
b What are the indications that O'Brien was Gammage's hero?
c Why was O'Brien mistaken about the effects of Free Trade?
d What was O'Brien's role in the movement up to 1848, and what
happened to him subsequently?

3 Bronterre O'Brien

At present the people may arm, both legally and constitutionally. It
may not be so legal to arm after the meeting of Parliament [February
1839]. The Parliament once assembled, and the people *unarmed*, the
National Convention will be about as powerful as forty-nine babes
5   in their swaddling clothes. . . .

Operative, 30 December 1838

If God sent the rich into the world with combs on their heads like
fighting cocks, if he sent the poor into the world with humps on their
backs like camels, then I would say that it was predestined that the
10 rich should be born booted and spurred, ready to ride over the poor;
but when I see that God made no distinction between rich and poor –
when I see that all men are sent into this working world without
silver spoons in their mouths or shirts on their backs, I am satisfied
that all must labour in order to get themselves fed and clothed. . . .
15 Unfortunately, those who have not worked themselves, whose
ancestors have never worked, have all the good things, while those
whose fathers and mothers have worked hard and who themselves
have all their lives worked hard, endure all the privations and
sufferings which can be inflicted in this world. . . . You produce
20 annually 450 millions of wealth, and the idlers take 4s 6d a pound of
it. They take nearly one-fourth, though they are only one in two
thousand of the people. Next come the profit-mongers – those who
make their fortunes by grinding the poor and cheating the rich . . .
who buy cheap and sell dear, who spoil [i.e. steal] the wholesome
25 articles you have made and distribute them to others – they take 7s 6d
a pound of what you produce. Thus 12s is gone before you have a
pick. They promise you a paradise hereafter. You pay 1s to the clergy
for that, on condition they preach to you to be content with your lot
and to be pleased with what divine providence has done for you. . . .
30 Then they take 2s 6d a pound for their military forces – to keep you

down. This leaves 4s 6d. . . . By God's help this system shall be changed before the year's end. . . .

Address on Monkton Moor, Scotland, 1839

Let the government dare to hang one Chartist – and for every one there would be ten of the other class hung up to their own doors
35 [Applause]. The question was, were they up to the mark and provided with the appliances wherewith to bring the accursed profit-mongers to their senses? [*Yes!*] He would not and durst not say anything illegal, because he heard that there were already 29 warrants of one sort or another out against different members of the
40 Convention; but he bade the labouring classes to . . . prove by hanging something bright and shining over their chimney pieces that they were prepared for the crisis. . . .

Address at Stockport, *Manchester Times*, 20 July 1839; *Northern Star*, 20 July 1839

Let not the anvil be struck within the breadth and length of the land. Let not a spade be used unless to dig some tyrant's grave. Let not a
45 shuttle move, unless to weave the winding sheet of some monster robber, some profit-monger, who dared to attack the people's Parliament. All will then soon be over.

Quoted in A. Plummer, *Bronterre*, 1971, pp 99, 117–18, 122

Questions

a What were the features which made O'Brien's speeches so powerful?
b Why might lines 19–31 be so effective to working-class audiences?
c Were these speeches inciting rebellion?
d On the basis of these documents discuss Thorne's comment that 'Fiery agitation, not patient propaganda, was the method of men like O'Brien and Harney'.

4 The English Marat

Vanity was one of his prevailing weaknesses. . . . We do not intend to cast a slight upon his talents, for they were considerable, but many men of respectable talents fall into the mistake of supposing themselves to be greater than they really are, and from this weakness
5 Harney was not free. . . . His dark piercing eyes were shaded by a rather moody brow, and were never at rest, but constantly changing from one object to another, as though he distrusted all around him. About his lips there was an appearance of strong vindictiveness, which pointed him out as a dangerous enemy, and experience only
10 served to prove the correctness of the impression. It may, however,

be said of him, that to those whom he considered his friends no man could be more warmly or devotedly attached. In the early part of his political life Harney aspired to be the Marat of the English Revolution, with whom, indeed, he was once charged with compar-
15   ing himself. His talent was best displayed when he wielded the pen; as a speaker he never came up to the standard of third class orators. . . . In a time of calm he would never as a speaker have succeeded in gaining a prominent position; but that was not a time of calm, – strong words were in brisk demand, and the masses cared for
20   little else. Harney had a sufficiency to stock the political market, and he was ever liberal in their use. . . .

Harney appeared [at the Birmingham Convention] to think that nothing but the most extreme measures were of the slightest value. He was moving towards the object by the speediest means, and he
25   seldom, if ever, stopped to calculate the cost. . . .

Gammage, op cit, pp 29–30, 109–10

Questions

a   Explain the reference that 'Harney aspired to be the Marat of the English Revolution' (lines 13–14).
b   Gammage seemed to pay particular attention to the facial characteristics of the Chartist leaders. Do you think that this has any validity in terms of their personalities?
c   'Force was Harney's watchword.' (C. Thorne) Examine the role of George Joshua Harney in the Chartist movement.

5   Moral and Physical Force (i)

We believe these discussions of moral and physical force were, generally speaking, a mere waste of time. We look upon the two kinds of force to be inseparably linked. In political matters, unquestionably so. Governments are necessarily institutions of
5   force, moral to a certain extent, but beyond that extent, physical. A government without physical force would be simply no government at all. . . . The law . . . should always be supported by a power physical in its nature, but founded on the moral opinion of the people, for without this it is a dead letter. . . . We might challenge the
10   history of the world to show that any government on earth, of an exclusive character, was ever moved to the abdication of its usurped functions except by physical force or the fear of it. . . . All threats of physical force should be avoided in every case, until the people are imbued with a sound knowledge of their political and social rights.
15   When so prepared, should their oppressors refuse to concede their claims, they will want but little admonishing, for the law of self-preservation will tell them what to do. . . . The war words of the moral and physical force reformers waxed warm on both sides; it did

not, however, for a time, detract seriously from the power of the
20 movement. . . and a considerable time elapsed before the split began
materially to operate to the weakness and injury of the radical party,
but that weakness and injury came at last.

> Gammage, op cit, pp 85–6

Questions

a Why did Gammage think 'the two kinds of force to be
inseparably linked' (lines 2–3)? Do you agree with his views?
b What were the steps in the nineteenth century by which 'the
people [became] imbued with a sound knowledge of their
political and social rights' (lines 13–14)? How much had been
achieved by 1854?
c Was Gammage correct when he wrote that 'a considerable time
elapsed before the split began materially to operate to the
weakness and injury of the radical party' (lines 20–1)?

6 Moral and Physical Force (ii)

Unhappily, the conflicting opinions entertained by some portion of
the working-classes regarding *the means* of accomplishing that object
have hitherto greatly retarded it; but we trust that experience, the
great teacher of mankind, has led them to perceive that no other
5   means are likely to be so effective as *a peaceful combination of the
millions*, founding their hopes on the might and influence of
intellectual and *moral progress*. Our feelings, at least, being in favour of
such a description of organization, have induced us to set forth the
advantages it would possess; – *first*, in causing great numbers to join
10   us who are politically indifferent, or entertain erroneous notions
respecting the objects and intentions of 'the Chartists'. . . . Discord
and folly have to some extent unhappily prevailed, for want of
sufficient investigation, but still Chartism has already been led by
knowledge beyond the crushing influence of irresponsible and
15   vindictive persecutors; and though prejudice and faction may
contend with it for a season, it is yet destined to become a great and
efficient instrument of moral and intellectual improvement. . . .

> W. Lovett and J. Collins, *Chartism – a new organization of the
> people*, 1840 (1969 edn, Leicester), pp v, 1

The resolution carried unanimously at the end of the meeting [at
Peep Green]: That this meeting, seeing the determination of the
20   Government to resist the just demands of the people, consider it an
imperative duty on every lover of freedom and his country to rally
round and stand or fall by that Charter, which will ultimately be the
conservator of their rights and liberties. . . . If this government
persist in resisting their just demands, they cannot be held answer-

25 able for the deeds of men driven to desperation by insult and
oppression. . . .
The Times, 21 May 1839

No man can doubt, on hearing O'Brien, that he has little faith in the
efficacy of moral agitation; and that he looks to a revolution to
overturn the present government. . . . Therein we differ. We think
30 moral agitation is quite adequate to gain the Charter; and . . . we do
not believe they [the people] will ever be got to act in sufficient
numbers to gain it by force. . . .
True Scotsman, 13 July 1839

Question

a Discuss the arguments on moral and physical force in these
documents. To what extent do they support the view that
Chartists disagreed more on methods than on aims?

7 The 1842 Petition

Now . . . for the substance of their petition in which there are one or
two good sentences, and a very large number of unaccountably
trashy ones. . . . It complains of a variety of particular grievances –
some real and remediable by act of Parliament, as the New Poor
5 Law, perhaps too the cruelties practised in the factories, and the riots
and corruption of elections; some of which are real enough, but are
either necessary conditions of human society, or of our own present
position, or else utterly beyond the reach of legislation as at present
understood; – as taxation, and therein particularly the national debt;
10 the contrast between the luxury of the rich and the poverty of the
working classes; the existing restrictions on popular meetings, a
police, and a standing army; – others, finally, which are either actual
blessings, or at least such things as are grievances only to the fancy,
or are counter-balanced by great and palpable benefits, as an
15 established church, the expenses of a Royal family, and the
monopoly (as they call it) of machinery, land, the means of
travelling, and transit – in other words property.
    But the great and fundamental object of their attack is the present
state of the representation. . . .
20   We are content with the . . . simple belief that the great question to
be settled by the House of Commons . . . is not how the people shall
be fully represented, but how they shall be well governed; – that
Governments do not rest their authority on the consent of the
people, but simply on their own established existence – that the
25 powers *that be* have a claim upon our allegiance because *they are*, – and
that we, born under their authority, receiving, before we have the
power to express assent or dissent, the benefits of their protection,

through our whole lives as unable to disclaim as they are to
withdraw those benefits, and finally specifically commanded by that
30   authority from which both they and we derive all such rights as
either of us possess to pay them honour and obedience, are thus
morally and religiously bound to accept such a definition of our
rights as is given us by the constitution under which we live, and
within these limits only, to exert ourselves for the development of all
35   its beneficial, and the extirpation of its pernicious principles. . . .
        The Times, 3 May 1842

Questions

a   Explain what you think *The Times* meant by lines 7–9
b   What is the distinction between 'how the people shall be fully
     represented' and 'how they shall be well governed' (lines 21–2)?
     Do you agree with the distinction in the context of (i) the early
     nineteenth century, and (ii) the late twentieth century?
c   Was Chartism too concerned with taxes, as suggested in the first
     paragraph?
d   What values did *The Times* support which made it hostile to
     Chartism?

8   Cross-Channel Chartism

TO ENGLISH WORKING-MEN

MY DEAR COUNTRYMEN

Expelled from France by the ferocious cries of the disciples of
'Fraternity', thrust out almost naked from the land to which I had
5   taken my share of English enterprise and skill, without even time
enough to gather my effects together or receive my arrears of wages,
I arrive in London, having for my voyage and journey from the coast
become indebted to the kindness of the English government. . . .
What is my astonishment, then, to find in England men wicked
10   enough or mad enough to attempt to induce you to imitate the
country I have left – to have a Revolution in England!
I thought that I, a victim to the brutal violence of physical force,
had, at all events, left it behind me, and placed the English Channel
between us; but the first thing I observe on my arrival is this very
15   same French doctrine of Fraternity, to which I am so much indebted,
parading the streets of London in the disguise of Chartism!
Chartism – at least Chartism such as it is preached in Fitzroy
Square – is nothing else but Republicanism! What Republicanism is,
I, at all events, have ascertained to my cost!
20   The Chartists will tell you they only want the 'six points;' but they
have already proved themselves to be something more than

champions in the cause of Reform, by holding tumultuous assemblies to intimidate the Legislature! Their policy is so clumsy, that their leaders openly speak of taking the Charter 'by force.' Their speeches and actions convince me they are nothing but Republicans; ay, and French Republicans, too. . . .

These Chartists imitate the French in everything. They are about to call a 'National Assembly;' – they have their 'National Convention' already. They cannot even find English names for their gatherings together! We have a pretty fair sample of their truth and modesty, when we see a few demagogues arrogate to themselves the name of National Assembly. But they will tell you, 'We represent 5,000,000.' Yes, five millions of 'Pugnoses!' but when was the franchise extended to *them*? The British Parliament, which has proclaimed our liberties for centuries, must hide its diminished head before this French Chartist abortion! Must it? . . .

I have no doubt the Chartists would give us universal suffrage, but they would destroy capital, and thereby ruin industry, if we agreed to their bloodthirsty way of managing matters. They would destroy more liberty than they created; they would yield England, by their own acknowledgments, up to the license of physical force. . . .

In speaking of the Chartists, of course I mean physical-force Chartists, as moral-force Chartists are only Reformers; but if any of the obloquy which I seek to attach to the name of physical-force Chartists should visit moral-force Chartists, let them remember that they have assumed a false name, a name which does not belong to them, and be silent! It is their punishment, who are only Reformers, for leaguing themselves with Revolutionists. Now that the speeches in the Convention have laid bare the designs of physical force, let moral force dissolve the partnership. . . .

In a Republic no one is safe long, so swiftly do contending factions succeed each other. No sooner is one raised up than it is destroyed by another more audacious. A Republic seems to me like a bedlam without keepers; for where violence is the only test of patriotism, who more patriotic than a madman? Let them deny it as they may, a Republic on the Parisian model is the form of government, or rather of license, which the Chartists cherish in the inmost core of their hearts. A Government of Terror, wielded by a small minority in the State, is the end to which all their speeches, all their writings, all their measures go! . . .

To conclude, my dear countrymen, if we need Reform, and are convinced we do so upon good and sufficient grounds, by the blessing of God we will obtain it in the good old English way, and in no other: let us leave Revolution to Paris and to the Chartists!

One of their moral-force leaders said, 'Capitalists are fed upon the bones of little children!' Do not hearken to such nonsense. Without capital there could be no wages. Take my advice, work and become capitalists yourselves! You will then know that capitalists live on

industry – that they *are* merely what your children may *become*, if *you*
70 yourselves are industrious and work – the inheritors of the saved-up
wages of labour! . . .

Remember, then, that whenever these Chartists talk of Liberty,
they mean the liberty of committing crimes; whenever of Equality,
that they are sure to be the first to give you a proof of it by becoming
75 your tyrants; whenever of Fraternity, that it is to the glorious
fraternal feelings of France that you are indebted for this exposure of
your most bitter enemies, the physical-force Chartists: for had it not
been for fraternity I should still have been at full work and full wages
in France, instead of being

80   Your humble Servant,
                          A POOR ARTISAN,
                 Without a Shilling in the World.

*What the Chartists Are. A Letter to English Working-Men by a
Fellow-Labourer*, 1848, pp 3–4, 6–8, 10–12

Questions

a   Explain: the references to France in lines 3–4 and 12; 'Chartism
    such as it is preached in Fitzroy Square' (lines 17–18); 'five
    millions of "Pugnoses"' (line 33).
b   Examine the validity of the writer's assertion throughout this
    pamphlet that 'their speeches and actions convince me they are
    nothing but Republicans . . .' (lines 24–5).
c   'This French Chartist abortion!' (line 36). In what ways did the
    Chartists consciously or unconsciously adopt aspects of the
    French Revolution?
d   'The license of physical force' (line 41). Was this the stick to beat
    the movement?
e   From any knowledge that you may have of mediaeval or early
    modern English history – especially the seventeenth century –
    comment on the conclusion that 'if we need Reform . . . we will
    obtain it in the good old English way . . .' (lines 61–3).
f   Was this returning Englishman in a good position to judge events
    in 1848?

9   The Chartist Circular

To those who live in large commercial districts, the effects of such a
publication will not be so obvious as to those who reside in the
obscure hamlet, or the farm cottage. People in populous towns have,
through the medium of libraries, reading rooms, and newspaper
5 societies, every opportunity of acquiring a considerable amount of
knowledge; although it is to be regretted that even in those places
there are to be found very many in such miserable circumstances,
that though they even felt inclined to read, they cannot afford the

means: to poor working men in that condition, a weekly perusal of
10 the *Circular* cannot fail to be both useful and gratifying. Besides
these, there are in large towns a class of keen and energetic minds,
who eagerly pore over the columns of their favourite newspapers – a
species of literature too deeply imbued in general with the rancorous
spirit of party politics to afford much solid information; readers of
15 this description . . . may peruse the calm argumentative articles of
the *Circular* with much advantage to themselves. It is, however, to
the working men of the humble *clachan*, or the thinly peopled parish
who seldom see a periodical of any kind but such as first passes
through the hands of the *laird*, the minister, or the merchant, who for
20 the most part only patronise the poisonous productions of the Tory
press as well in politics as religion: it is to working men in
circumstances like these who have been in the habit of drawing their
information from such corrupt sources, that the *Chartist Circular*
sheds a stream of new light. . . .
25   It has been widely circulated in most of our large districts –
arousing the apathetic, – animating the timid, – restraining the
imprudent, and enlightening the ignorant as it moved on. But what
is still more gratifying, it has formed a large circle of acquaintance
among the hills and glens of Scotland – a circle who, prior to its
30 introduction, had never heard of the People's Charter. . . . Various
are the incidents which have brought it to the dwellings of our rustic
brethren. The pedlar, stooping beneath his ponderous shoulder-
establishment, may be seen wending his way to a group of cottages,
in some of which he regales the brawny blacksmith, the loquacious
35 shoemaker, or the polite tailor, with a world's news, and ends his
edifying discourse by exhibiting, amongst his various wares, a few
numbers of the *Circular*. It was in this very way that it found its road to
a large mountainous tract of country, in which we spent most of our
early days; and though it is now widely diffused there, yet in our
40 recollection, and we are not very old, no papers were read there but
one, and that one was a Tory gem of the first water. Indeed, so
tranquilly did the inhabitants of that sequestered district plod on in
the depths of unconscious slavery, that we do not remember them
ever taking a part in politics but once, and that was at the abdication
45 of Napoleon, when they broke the village bell in the plenitude of
their rejoicings. Agitation was a word they knew not, and seldom
felt except at a goblin story, or when a furious thunderstorm, or a
piece of still more furious pulpit oratory, which seldom happened,
disturbed their equanimity. But now, to the horror and mortification
50 no doubt, of the patron and the priest, they have, thanks to our
present movement and its auxiliaries, fixed their gaze at last upon their
fetters, and are panting for the liberty of freemen. . . . In the words of
the immortal La Fayette, 'For a Nation to love liberty, it is sufficient
that she knows it, and to be free, it is sufficient that she wills it.' It was
55 to promote to the utmost extent of their limited means that

knowledge, that the Central Committee instituted the Circular; and had they been furnished with funds sufficient to employ national lecturers, they would, through the energies of their faithful and enlightened missionaries, have been enabled to direct against the
60   batteries of corruption the whole artillery of their moral strength. . . .

WILLIAM THOMSON

> *The Chartist Circular* published under the Superintendence of the Universal Suffrage Central Committee for Scotland, dedicated to the Victims of Legislative Oppression! The Industrial Millions of the Kingdom of Great Britain and Ireland, Preface, v, 23 October 1841

Questions

a   Why did the *Chartist Circular* believe Chartist newspapers to be invaluable?

b   Against whom in Scotland did this newspaper struggle most?

c   Which arguments or expressions suggest a romanticised view of political emancipation in Scotland?

d   What educational and transport developments in the first half of the nineteenth century made newspapers more accessible to ordinary people?

10   The *Northern Star*

Never was a journal started more opportunely. It caught and reflected the spirit of the times. . . . *The Northern Star* speedily stood at the head of the democratic journals. Its editor was the Rev. William Hill, an acute and clever but not a very agreeable writer. . . . Two
5 circumstances contributed to raise it in popular estimation. One of these was the popularity of O'Connor, a popularity which was largely due to the fact of his having a journal in which to record all his proceedings and to place his words and deeds in the most advantageous light. The other . . . was, that the *Star* was regarded as the most
10 complete record of the movement. There was not a meeting held in any part of the country, in however remote a spot, that was not reported in its columns, accompanied by all the flourishes calculated to excite an interest in the readers' mind, and to inflate the vanity of the speakers by the honourable mention of their names. Even if they
15 had never mounted the platform before, the speeches were described and reported as eloquent, argumentative, and the like. . . . Thus men of very mediocre abilities appeared to people at a distance to be oracles of political wisdom. . . .

What also gave it an advantage over other papers was the spirit
20 which pervaded its columns. So far from propounding the moral force sentiments of the *London Despatch* it enforced doctrines of the

very opposite tendency. O'Connor in his speeches had so inflamed the public mind that it had become almost insatiable, and the *Star* endeavoured to supply what was wanting. Its pages were read every
25 week with surprising eagerness, and at every draught the fever increased; to appease their thirst its readers drank deeper than before, until they were seized with a kind of delirium, and nothing that did not savour of physical force stood the slightest chance of being swallowed by the vast majority. . . .

Gammage, op cit, pp 16–18

Questions

a   What three circumstances, in Gammage's opinion, contributed to the success of the *Northern Star*?
b   Who was the chief beneficiary of the paper, and why?
c   Using extracts from the *Northern Star* in other sections, examine 'the spirit which pervaded its columns' (lines 19–20).
d   If an historian read an account of an event in *The Times* and the *Northern Star* would he or she judge the truth to lie midway between the two?

11   The Condition of England

A feeling very generally exists that the condition and disposition of the Working Classes is a rather ominous matter at present; that something ought to be said, something ought to be done, in regard to it. And surely, at an epoch of history when the 'National Petition'
5   carts itself in waggons along the streets, and is presented 'bound with iron hoops, four men bearing it', to a reformed House of Commons; and Chartism numbered by the million and half, taking nothing by its iron-hooped Petition, breaks out into brickbats, cheap pikes, and even into sputterings of conflagration, such very general feeling
10 cannot be considered unnatural! To us individually this matter appears, and has for many years appeared, to be the most ominous of all practical matters whatever; a matter in regard to which if something be not done, something will *do* itself one day, and in a fashion that will please nobody. The time is verily come for acting in
15 it; how much more for consultation about acting in it, for speech and articulate inquiry about it!

We are aware that, according to the newspapers, Chartism is extinct; that a Reform Ministry has 'put down the chimera of Chartism' in the most felicitous effectual manner. So say the
20 newspapers; – and yet, alas, most readers of newspapers know withal that it is indeed the 'chimera' of Chartism, not the reality, which has been put down. The distracted incoherent embodiment of Chartism, whereby in late months it took shape and became visible, this has been put down; or rather has fallen down and gone asunder by

25   gravitation and law of nature: but the living essence of Chartism has
not been put down. Chartism means the bitter discontent grown
fierce and mad, the wrong condition therefore or the wrong
disposition, of the Working Classes of England. It is a new name for a
thing which has had many names, which will yet have many. The
30   matter of Chartism is weighty, deep-rooted, far-extending; did not
begin yesterday; will by no means end this day or to-morrow.
Reform Ministry, constabulary rural police, new levy of soldiers,
grants of money to Birmingham; all this is well, or is not well; all this
will put down only the embodiment or 'chimera' of Chartism. The
35   essence continuing, new and ever new embodiments, chimeras
madder or less mad, have to continue. The melancholy fact remains,
that this thing known at present by the name Chartism does exist;
has existed; and either 'put down', into secret treason, with rusty
pistols, vitriol-bottle and match-box, or openly brandishing pike
40   and torch . . . is like to exist till quite other methods have been tried
with it. What means this bitter discontent of the Working Classes?
Whence comes it, whither goes it? Above all, at what price, on what
terms, will it probably consent to depart from us and die into rest?
These are questions.
45   To say that it is mad, incendiary, nefarious, is no answer. . . .
Glasgow Thuggery, Chartist torch-meetings, Birmingham riots,
Swing conflagrations, are so many symptoms on the surface; you
abolish the symptom to no purpose, if the disease is left
untouched. . . .
50   Delirious Chartism will not have raged entirely to no purpose, as
indeed no earthly thing does so, if it have forced all thinking men of
the community to think of this vital matter, too apt to be overlooked
otherwise.

      T. Carlyle, *Chartism*, 1840, pp 1–3, quoted in Gash, op cit, pp
      103–5

Questions

a   Explain the references to: 'National Petition' (line 4); 'reformed
    House of Commons' (line 6); 'Swing conflagrations' (line 47).
b   How did Carlyle distinguish between the reality and chimera
    (line 21) of Chartism?
c   'The matter of Chartism is weighty, deep-rooted, far-extending;
    did not begin yesterday; will by no means end this day or
    to-morrow' (lines 29–31). What 'condition of England' was
    Carlyle trying to impress upon his readers, and how were these
    problems resolved during the nineteenth and twentieth cen-
    turies?
d   Which elements of thought and expression made Thomas
    Carlyle one of the notable political philosophers of the period?

V The Plug Plot, 1842

Introduction

The 'Plug Plot' disturbances of 1842 were not Chartist inspired, but it is vital to ask at what point they were taken over by the Chartists. The background is of trade depression in the textile and metal industries, with trade groups trying unsuccessfully to prevent wage reductions. The co-ordinated threat to pull out the plugs from the steam engine boilers was serious, and lends credence to the view of several historians that this was in reality a general strike.

The riot in Preston was on familiar lines with Mayor, magistrates and police receiving support from the army, although the Home Secretary's congratulations to the Mayor after this 'mad insurrection' were controversial.

The involvement of Thomas Cooper was an indication of Chartist support, but local leaders like Richard Pilling were equally important. As in 1839, social conditions were bad. More than half the sixty cotton mills in Bolton were closed or on short time, 10,000 Boltonians were receiving parish relief; one house in six was empty, and many families had no furniture left of any kind. The *Illustrated London News* reported the attack on the Stockport Union workhouse; according to Engels, workhouses 'were the favourite child of the bourgeoisie'. Strong responses came from Tory newspapers, and Edward Baines – a noted local historian as well as editor of the *Leeds Mercury* – wrote in favour of the millowners.

As Christopher Thorne has commented, 'the renewed activity of 1842 . . . was quick to fade. . . . Many in the North of England returned to the attack on the Poor Law. Others took up the Ten-Hour cause again. . . .'

Yet social distress remained, M. Faucher, visiting Bolton in 1844, 'visited 1,000 families containing 5,305 individuals. The average wages did not exceed 10d. per head, they had amongst them only 1,553 beds . . . and the half of these were without mattresses, and were filled only with straw or rags; 53 families had no bed, and 425 persons slept on the floor. . . .'

Was it really the trade-cycle and not Chartism which could alleviate this distress?

1 The Plug Plot

We have to record the disastrous occurrence of a turn-out of manufacturing labourers in and about Manchester, which must be regarded with sorrow by wise and thoughtful men. It would appear that the sudden and turbulent display of congregated thousands,

5   leaving their daily employment – marching upon mills, forcing willing and unwilling alike to join them and, in a moment, paralysing the whole activity of the natural enterprise of their neighbourhood, – arose, in the first instance, from a reduction of wages in one quarter, given almost without notice, and taken by the

10 men as the omen of a general intention on the part of the masters everywhere else. At once, with a desperation of purpose, they gathered in half-starved thousands, resolved to abjure work, unless they can have 'a fair day's pay for a fair day's labour'; and partly with riot, partly with invective, partly with threat, plunged the sober

15 population into fear, and created anxieties, natural to these troublous times, from one end to the other of the land.

All the manufacturing districts have been up in arms; at Preston the insurgents were fired upon, and some of them wounded mortally. At Stockport, where there are upwards of 20,000 persons

20 out of employment who have no resources but those of plunder and beggary, a large body of rioters broke open and pillaged the workhouses of food and clothing, and mobs robbed the provision shops. Troops, guards, and artillery have been poured in upon the shocking scene of insurrection; and there seems to have been a

25 spreading organisation of a most formidable and disciplined character. The fact that troops had been ordered to the disturbed districts soon became publicly known, and produced an intense feeling of alarm and excitement in the mind of individuals generally.

The anti-corn-law leaguer and the chartist are, we fear, respon-

30 sible for these agitations – responsible, as we think, to their Queen, their country, and their God. We are no partisans; we do not oppose, abstractedly for their peculiar doctrines, either the chartist or the anti-corn-law leaguer; we leave all political opinion, however violent, its fair play; but we despise the infamous diplomacy which

35 would make its game out of the miseries of the people. Nothing can more excite our indignant rebuke than the revolutionary villain or the quack preacher of politics, who says, 'I have a charter to achieve here, or a corn-law to repeal there, and, now that the people are starving and in tatters, I will convert their rags into banners of

40 rebellion, and their hunger into the sign of blood.' Yet this, we believe, is the course that was pursued, furnishing the key to all the riots and seditions that disturbed the land.

The more remarkable features of the proceedings at Stockport were the extortion of money from mill-owners as well as shop-keepers,

45 and an attack on the New Union Workhouse, Shaw-heath, where

the mob forced an entrance and immediately commenced to help themselves to bread and money. Information of this was conveyed to the authorities, and they hastened to the spot with the constables, and infantry, and captured about forty of the rioters.

Illustrated London News, August 1842

Questions

a   Why were the people of the North West of England 'starving and in tatters' (line 39) in 1842?

b   Why was an attack made on the Stockport Workhouse (lines 21–2, 45–9)?

c   How did the authorities try to prevent disorder?

d   'We are no partisans' (line 31). Do you agree?

e   Does the journal produce evidence for stating that 'there seems to have been a spreading organisation of a most formidable and disciplined character' (lines 24–6)?

f   What were the links between Chartism and the Anti-Corn Law League?

2   The Crisis

Resolution of the metal trades conference, Thursday 11 August 1842
I That this meeting pledges itself not to sanction any illegal or immoral proceedings.

II That this meeting deprecates the late and present conduct of those
5   employers who have been reducing wages; thereby depriving the labourers of the means of subsistence, and also destroying the home trade; but at the same time we can not, nor do we sanction the conduct of those individuals who have been going about destroying property, and offering violence to the people.
10   III That it is the opinion of this meeting that, until class legislation is entirely destroyed, and the principle of united labour is established, the labourer will not be in a position to enjoy the fruits of his own industry.

IV That it is the opinion of this meeting the people's charter ought
15   to become the law of the land, as it contains the elements of justice and prosperity; and we pledge ourselves never to relinquish our demands until that document becomes a legislative enactment.

V That a committee be appointed by this meeting, to wait upon the other trades, to endeavour, if possible, to secure a more general
20   union, before entering into any practical measures for redressing any grievances.

VI That a committee be appointed to draw up an address to employers in general, showing them the evil results of reducing wages.
25   VII That the trades now assembled do pledge themselves not to

commence work until they have had an interview with deputations from other trades.

VIII That the foregoing resolutions be printed, and posted in different parts of the town and neighbourhood. . . .

30 **Address of the metal trades conference, Friday 12 August 1842**
An adjourned public meeting of the mechanics, engineers, mill-wrights, moulders and smiths was held on Friday afternoon . . . in the Carpenters' Hall to take into consideration the best means to be adopted at the present alarming crisis. . . .

35 1 That we the delegates, representing the various trades of Manches-ter and its vicinities with delegates from various parts of Lancashire and Yorkshire, do most emphatically declare that it is our solemn and conscientious conviction, that all the evils that afflict society and which have prostrated the energies of the great body of the

40 producing classes, arise solely from class legislation; and that the only remedy for the present alarming distress and widespread destitution is the immediate and unmutilated adoption and carrying into law, the document known as the People's Charter.

2 That a trades' delegate meeting be held at the Sherwood Inn, Tib

45 Street, on Monday, 15 August . . . to which every trade in Manchester is particularly requested to send a delegate to represent its opinions at the present truly important crisis. And that this meeting pledges itself not to commence work again until such delegates have come to a decision; and likewise call upon all other

50 trades who have ceased labour to remain out till that time. . . .

4 That this meeting individually and collectively pledges itself to become the conservators of the peace, discountenance the destruc-tion of property, and will assist to arrest any whom they find trying to create a breach of the peace.

55 5 That this meeting begs of the working classes not to use intoxicating drinks until the people's charter becomes the law of the land. . . .

Questions

a   What recent events were referred to in lines 8–9?
b   What steps was the metal trades conference seeking to take? Were they to be peaceful or violent?
c   Which parliamentary acts of the early nineteenth century could be construed as 'class legislation' (lines 10, 40)?
d   What social *and* financial benefits was the conference expecting from resolution 5 (lines 55–7)?
e   Are there comparisons to be drawn between these meetings and a late-twentieth-century trade dispute?

3 Violence in Preston

(a) On the 12th of August a meeting was held at Preston. . . . On the following morning, as early as five o'clock, a crowd had assembled . . . they moved off in order to stop a factory that was still working. From this factory they proceeded to others; but while the people
5 were busy, the authorities were by no means idle. The magistrates met and ordered out the police, as well as thirty of the 72nd Highlanders who were quartered in the town. The magistrates accompanied the soldiers down Fishergate, where they met an immense number of persons whom they prevented from passing up
10 the street. Proceeding down Fishergate and Lune-street the soldiers were pelted by the people with showers of stones, upon which they faced about with the view of effecting a dispersion, which they made great efforts to accomplish. The chief of the county constabulary told them that the Riot Act would be read; but a stone was immediately
15 thrown, which knocked the Riot Act out of the Mayor's hand. Showers of stones flew from all sides at the military. The Mayor, however, succeeded at last in reading the Riot Act. . . . Women filled their aprons with stones, and brought them to the men. . . . It was in vain that the soldiers attempted to disperse them. All attempts to do
20 so by a mere display of force were ineffectual, and the Mayor at last gave the order to fire. At the first discharge many of the people fell to the ground; the rest did not run away, but stood for two or three minutes in a state of consternation. . . . Four were shot dead, and many others were wounded. The remainder speedily dispersed. . . .

> Gammage, op cit, p 221

(b) At length the mayor ordered the soldiers to fire. I did not hear what was the word of command; but they did fire.
What was the consequence of the firing?
I saw several of the foremost of the mob drop in the street.
5 How many rounds did they fire?
I don't know the exact number; they did not fire in a body but by platoons. The mob stood mute; they did not attempt to run; they stood for some minutes as if thunder-struck.
How long did they stand?
10 About two or three minutes.
I believe some were killed?
Yes.
How many?
Four died ultimately and a fifth man who was wounded had his leg
15 taken off.

> Evidence of the Chief Constable of Preston at the trial of Feargus O'Connor and 58 others

The unlawful assembly . . . proceeded with great violence to assault

the persons who had so come to disperse them, and knocked down
John Woodford, Chief Constable of the County of Lancaster . . .
threw stones and other missiles at the said mayor. . . . In defence of
20 themselves [the soldiers] justifiably and necessarily fired upon the
said offenders with musketry. . . .
   Verdict of the Coroner's Court

I assert that the mayor behaved with the utmost courage, he was
present during the whole of the proceedings when the troops were
attacked, and when they fired and he exercised his civil authority, not
25 ordering the firing to commence till the danger had become
imminent, and causing the firing to close when the danger had been
overcome. By the conduct of the chief magistrate the effusion of
human blood was stopped, and I may state that the town was
satisfied with the conduct of that chief officer; for if I am not
30 mistaken, the Mayor has received the thanks of the citizens for his
conduct.
   Sir James Graham, Home Secretary. *Parliamentary Debates*,
   3rd series, vol 68, col 122, quoted in M. Jenkins, *The General
   Strike of 1842*, 1980, pp 96–101

Questions

a How might Gammage have obtained his information?
b 'Justifiably and necessarily' (Document b, line 20). Do you agree?
  Why was Sir James Graham's speech badly received in some
  quarters?
c What problems do events like this pose for the historian?

4 A Royal Proclamation

BY THE QUEEN
A PROCLAMATION

VICTORIA R.

WHEREAS

5 In divers parts of Great Britain great Multitudes of lawless and
disorderly Persons have lately assembled themselves together in a
riotous and tumultuous manner, and have, with Force and Violence,
entered into certain Mines, Mills, Manufactories, and other Places,
and have, by Threats and Intimidation, prevented our good Subjects
10 therein employed from following their usual occupations and
earning their Livelihood; We, therefore, being duly sensible of the
MISCHIEVOUS CONSEQUENCES which must inevitably ensue, as
well to the Peace of the Kingdom as to the Lives and Properties of
our Subjects, from such wicked and illegal practices if they go

15   unpunished, and being firmly resolved to cause the laws to be put in
execution for the PUNISHMENT OF SUCH OFFENDERS, have thought
fit by the advice of our Privy Council, to issue this proclamation,
hereby strictly commanding all Justices of the Peace, Sheriffs, Under
Sheriffs and all other Civil Officers whatsoever within the said
20   Kingdom, that they do use their utmost endeavours to discover,
apprehend, and bring to Justice, the Persons concerned in the riotous
proceedings above mentioned: And as a further inducement to
discover the said offenders, We do hereby promise and declare, that
any person or persons who shall DISCOVER AND APPREHEND, or
25   cause to be discovered and apprehended, the authors abettors, or
perpetrators, of any of the outrages above mentioned, so that they or
any of them may be duly convicted thereof, shall be entitled to the
Sum of FIFTY POUNDS, for each and every person who shall be so
convicted, and shall also receive our most gracious pardon for the
30   said offence in case the person making such discovery as aforesaid
shall be liable to be prosecuted for the same.
Given at our Court at Windsor, this Thirteenth Day of August, in the
year of Our Lord one thousand eight hundred and forty-two, and in
the sixth year of our reign.
35   GOD SAVE THE QUEEN.

Questions

a   Do lines 5–11 provide a valid explanation of the events of the
'Plug Plot'?
b   Was the system of law officers (lines 18–19) sufficient for a
dispute of this scale?
c   Discuss the advantages and disadvantages of paying and pardon-
ing informants (lines 24–31).
d   What was Queen Victoria's personal opinion of the Chartists and
their aims?

5   Thomas Cooper

'The Plug Plot', of 1842, as it is still called in Lancashire, began in
reductions of wages by the Anti-Corn-Law manufacturers, who did
not conceal their purpose of driving the people to desperation, in
order to paralyse the Government. The people advanced at last, to a
5   wild general strike, and drew the plugs so as to stop the works at the
mills, and thus render labour impossible. Some wanted the men who
spoke at the meetings held at the beginning of the strike to propose
resolutions in favour of Corn Law Repeal; but they refused. The first
meeting where the resolution was passed, 'that all labour should
10   cease until the People's Charter became the law of the land', was held
on the 7th of August, on Mottram Moor. In the course of a week, the

resolution had been passed in nearly all the great towns of Lancashire, and tens of thousands had held up their hands in favour of it. . . .

15   [Cooper was in Hanley, in the Potteries, on the 15th August] By six o'clock, thousands crowded into the large open space about the Crown Inn. . . . Before I began, some of the men who were drunk, and who, it seems, had been in the riot at Longton, came round me and wanted to shake hands with me. But I shook them off, and told

20   them I was ashamed to see them. I began by telling the immense crowd. . . . that I had heard there had been destruction of property that day, and I warned all who had participated in that act, that they were not the friends, but the enemies of freedom – that ruin to themselves and others must attend this strike for the Charter, if they

25   who pretended to be its advocates broke the law. . . .

At dusk, I closed the meeting; but I saw the people did not disperse; and two pistols were fired off in the crowd. No policeman had I seen the whole day! And what had become of the soldiers I could not learn. . . . My friends had purposely conducted me

30   through dark streets, and led me out of Hanley in such a way that I saw neither spark, smoke, or flame. Yet the rioters were burning the houses of the Rev. Mr Aitken and Mr Parker, local magistrates, and the house of Mr Forrester, agent of Lord Granville (principal owner of the collieries in the Potteries) during the night. . . . Next morning

35   thousands were again in the streets of Hanley and began to pour into the other Pottery towns from the surrounding districts. A troop of cavalry . . . entered the district and the daring colliers strove to unhorse the soldiers. Their commander reluctantly gave the order to fire; one man was killed at Burslem. The mob dispersed; but quiet

40   was not restored until the day after . . . and scores apprehended and taken to prison.

When I entered the railway carriage at Crewe, some who were going to the Convention recognised me. . . . So soon as the City of Long Chimneys came in sight, and every chimney was beheld

45   smokeless, Campbell's [Secretary of the National Charter Association] face changed, and with an oath he said, 'Not a single mill at work! something must come out of this, and something serious too!'. . . .

In the streets, there was unmistakable signs of alarm on the part of

50   the authorities. Troops of cavalry were going up and down the principal thoroughfares, accompanied by pieces of artillery, drawn by horses. In the evening, we held a meeting in the Reverend Mr Schofield's chapel, where O'Connor, the Executive, and a considerable number of delegates were present. . . . There were nearly sixty

55   delegates present; and as they rose, in quick succession, to describe the state of their districts, it was evident they were. . . . filled with the desire of keeping the people from returning to their labour. They believed the time had come for trying, successfully, to paralyse the

Government. I caught their spirit – for the working of my mind had
60 prepared me for it. . . .
When the Executive, and a few others, had spoken, all in favour of
the universal strike, I told the Conference I should vote for the
resolution because it meant fighting, and I saw it must come to that.
The spread of the strike would and must be followed by a general
65 outbreak. The authorities of the land would try to quell it, but we
must resist them. There was nothing now but a physical force
struggle to be looked for. We must get the people out to fight; and
they must be irresistible, if they were united. . . .
O'Connor spoke late – evidently waiting to gather the spirit of the
70 meeting before he voted with the majority, which he meant to do
from the first. Yet he meant to do nothing in support of the strike,
although he voted for it!
McDouall was a different kind of spirit. He hastily drew up an
exciting and fiercely worded address to the working men of
75 England, appealing to the God of Battles for the issue, and urging a
universal strike. He got Leach to print this before the Convention
broke up in the evening. . . .

> *Life of Thomas Cooper, written by himself*, 1879, pp 190–211,
> quoted in N. Gash (ed), *The Age of Peel*, 1968, pp 99–103

Questions

a   How did the 'Plug Plot' acquire its name?
b   Why was Cooper at the Crown, Hanley (line 17)? What action
    did he urge upon the crowd, whose houses did the rioters attack
    first, and why?
c   Discuss the influence on the events described here of:
        (i)   Chartist leaders;
        (ii) the army;
        (iii) railways;
        (iv) nonconformity.
d   Why did Cooper decide to support the strike?
e   What impression of O'Connor does Cooper provide? How does
    it compare with those offered in Chapter IV?
f   What critical faculties would an historian employ when consider-
    ing Cooper's account as evidence?

6   A Call to Action!

Address of the executive committee of the National Charter Association, 17 August 1842

To the People

Brother Chartists – The great political truths which have been
5 agitated during the last half-century have *at length aroused* the

degraded and insulted white slaves of England to a sense of their duty
to themselves, their children, and their country. Tens of thousands
have flung down their implements of labour. Your taskmasters
tremble at your energy, and expecting masses eagerly watch this the
10   great crisis of our cause. Labour must no longer be the common prey
of masters and rulers. Intelligence has beamed upon the mind of the
bondsman, and he has been convinced that all wealth, comfort, and
produce, everything valuable, useful, and elegant, have sprung from
the palms of his hands; he feels that his cottage is empty, his back
15   thinly clad, his children breadless, himself hopeless, his mind
harassed, and his body punished, that *undue riches*, luxury, and
gorgeous plenty might be heaped on the palaces of the taskmasters,
and flooded in the granaries of the oppressor. Nature, God, and
reason, have condemned this inequality, and in the thunder of a
20   people's voice it must perish for ever. He knows that labour, the real
property of society, the sole origin of accumulated property, the first
cause of national wealth, and the only supporter, defender, and
contributor to the greatness of our country, is *not possessed of the same
legal protection which is given to those lifeless effects*, the houses, ships,
25   and machinery, which labour alone have created. He knows that if
labour has no protection, wages cannot be upheld nor in the slightest
degree regulated, until every workman of twenty-one years of age,
and of sane mind, is on the *same political level as the employer*. He
knows that the Charter would remove by universal will, expressed
30   in universal suffrage, the heavy load of taxes which now crush the
existence of the labourer, and cripple the effects of commerce; that it
would give cheap government as well as cheap food, high wages as
well as low taxes, bring happiness to the hearthstone, plenty to the
table, protection to the old, education to the young, permanent
35   prosperity to the country, long-continued protective political power
to labour, and peace, blessed peace, to exhausted humanity and
approving nations; therefore it is that we have solemnly sworn, and
one and all declared, that the golden opportunity now within our
grasp shall not pass away fruitless, that the chance of centuries
40   afforded to us by a wise and all-seeing God, shall not be lost; but that
we now do universally resolve never to resume labour until labour's
grievances are destroyed, and protection secured for ourselves, our
suffering wives, and helpless children, by the enactment of the
People's Charter.
45   Englishmen! the blood of your brothers reddens the streets of
Preston and Blackburn, and the murderers thirst for more. Be firm,
be courageous, be men. Peace, law, and order have prevailed on our
side – let them be revered until your brethren in Scotland, Wales, and
Ireland are informed of your resolution; and when the universal
50   holiday prevails, which will be the case in eight days, then of what
use will bayonets be against public opinion? What tyrant can then
live above the terrible tide of thought and energy, which is now

flowing fast, under the guidance of man's intellect, which is now
destined by a Creator to elevate his people above the reach of want,
55 the rancour of despotism, and the penalties of bondage. The trades, a
noble, patriotic band, have taken the lead in declaring for the
Charter, and drawing their gold from the keeping of tyrants. Follow
their example. Lend no whip to rulers wherewith to scourge you.

Intelligence has reached us of the widespreading of the strike, and
60 now, within fifty miles of Manchester, every engine is at rest, and all
is still, save the miller's useful wheels and the friendly sickle in the
fields.

Countrymen and brothers, centuries may roll on as they have
fleeted past, before such universal action may again be displayed; we
65 have made the cast for liberty, and we must stand, like men, the
hazard of the die. Let none despond. Let all be cool and watchful; and,
like the bridesmaids in the parable, keep your lamps burning; and
let continued resolution be like a beacon to guide those who
are now hastening far and wide to follow your memorable
70 example. . . .

Our machinery is all arranged, and your cause will, in three days,
be impelled onward by all the intellect we can summon to its aid;
therefore, whilst you are peaceful, be firm; whilst you are orderly,
make all be so likewise; and whilst you look to the law, remember
75 that you had no voice in making it, and are therefore the slaves to the
will, the law, and the price of your masters.

All officers of the association are called upon to aid and assist in the
peaceful extension of the movement, and to forward all monies for
the use of the delegates who may be expressed over the country.
80 Strengthen our hands at this crisis. Support your leaders. Rally round
our sacred cause, and leave the decision to the God of justice and of
battle.

Quoted in Jenkins, op cit, pp 270–2

Questions

a What were 'the great political truths which have been agitated
during the last half-century' (lines 4–5)?
b How valid was the assertion of lines 7–8?
c Explain 'drawing their gold from the keeping of tyrants' (line
57).
d Was the Charter seen here as a means to an end, and what ends
were suggested?
e Which features made this address an effective rallying cry? Why
then did the 'Plug Plot' fail?
f What events in Europe since 1945 suggest, at least in the short
term, that lines 50–5 were over-optimistic?

Table 1   *Local Chartist speakers in Stalybridge–Ashton–Hyde, 26 July–7 August*

Meetings		Speakers			Chartists			
Date	Place	Name	Town	Occupation	Chartist	Del. to Chartist conf	One of 59	Del. to trades conf
26 July	Thacker's Foundry, Ashton	Woodruffe	Ashton	Cordwainer	x			x
		Aitken	Ashton	Schoolmaster	x	x	x	
		Pilling	Ashton	Weaver	x		x	
29 July	Haigh, Stalybridge	Fenton	Stalybridge	Shoemaker	x		x	
		Challenger	Ashton	Weaver	x		x	
		Brophy	Ashton	Chartist lecturer	x		x	
		Storah		Weaver	x		x	
		Stephenson	Stalybridge	Weaver	x		x	
1 August	Sportmen's Inn, Hyde	Candelet	Hyde	Fact operative	x		x	x
		Muirhouse	Hyde	Bellman	x		x	
		Wilde (Robt.)	Hyde		x		x	
		Leach (John)	Hyde	Tailor	x		x	
2 or 3 August	Hall Green, Dukinfield	Pilling	Ashton	Weaver	x		x	
		Challenger	Ashton	Weaver	x		x	
		Stephenson	Stalybridge		x		x	
		Storah	Ashton	Weaver	x		x	
		Wilde (R)						
5 August (a.m.)	Haigh (Bayley workers)	Fenton	Stalybridge	Shoemaker	x		x	
		Mahon	Stalybridge	Shoemaker	x	x	x	
		Durham	Stalybridge	Shoemaker	x		x	
		Stephenson	Stalybridge		x		x	

Meetings		Speakers			Chartists			
Date	Place	Name	Town	Occupation	Chartist	Del. to Chartist conf.	One of 59	Del. to trades conf.
5 August (evening)	Haigh (Bayley workers)	Fenton	Stalybridge	Shoemaker	x		x	
		Mahon			x		x	
		Durham			x		x	
		Stephenson	Stalybridge	Chartist lect.	x		x	
		Brophy			x		x	
6 August (evening)	Haigh	Fenton	Stalybridge	Shoemaker	x		x	
		Mahon	Stalybridge	Shoemaker	x	x	x	
		Durham	Stalybridge	Shoemaker	x		x	
		Stephenson	Stalybridge	Shoemaker	x		x	
		Brophy	Stalybridge	Chartist lect.	x		x	
7 August 10.30 a.m.	Mottram Moor	Muirhouse	Hyde	Bellman	x			
		Candelet	Hyde	Fact operative	x		x	x
		Wilde (R)					x	
		Stephenson	Stalybridge	Shoemaker	x		x	
7 August 2 p.m.	Mottram Moor	Muirhouse	Hyde	Bellman	x			
		Candelet	Hyde	Fact operative	x		x	x
		Wilde (R)					x	
		Stephenson	Stalybridge	Shoemaker	x		x	
		Storah	Ashton	Weaver	x		x	
		Mahon	Stalybridge	Shoemaker	x	x	x	
		Leach (J)	Hyde	Tailor	x		x	
		Crossley	Stalybridge			x		

Jenkins, op cit, pp 242–3

What hypotheses about Chartist speakers can be deduced from this table?

8   The Plug Plot on Trial: Richard Pilling

I am not one of those who would, like the Irish, live on lumpers – nor would I be, like a degraded Russian serf, sold with the land. I want to see the people here well educated, and if a man has the means in his pocket he will get his children educated; and if the people are once
5   well informed, then the Charter will be the law of the land. . . . And now Gentlemen of the Jury, you have the case before you; the masters conspired to kill me and I combined to keep myself alive. . . .
Richard Pilling's speech at his trial, March 1843

Mr Richard Pilling in introducing the next resolution exhorted the people to support the Convention and the Charter, attacked the
10   profligate expenditure of a Government professing retrenchment and no patronage, reviewed the cheerless condition of our foreign and home policy and the disheartening state of trade and the general state of the comforts of the people. Had the working people been in the legislature by their Charter this Nation would now have been the
15   most prosperous nation in the world. The working people as the origin of the arts, improvements, ingenuity and wealth, of the empires are the only fit persons to govern this or any other nation. The people will never be happy until then and I hope the working people will stand by the convention to obtain the Charter morally if
20   they can, but have it we will (*'Hear, hear'* and *'by arms'*) . . . the Chairman says I am out of order, therefore I will no longer trespass upon your time than by calling upon the working people to support the Charter. . . . I say the Charter, the Charter, and the Charter we'll have. . . .
Deposition to Lord John Russell re a Chartist meeting, Stockport, 11 May 1839, quoted in Jenkins, op cit, pp 110–12

25   Fellow Townsmen, for I may so call you having lived amongst you so long and having been at so many meetings attended by thousands, and having been in prison, I do not know whether it would be safe for me to own it or not; but I may avow that I have the honour to be the father of this movement and the sole cause of your being ladies
30   and gentlemen at the present time; for the masters of Ashton had thought proper to offer a reduction of 25 per cent upon their wages. I then caused the bellman to go round and call the meeting swearing by the God of Heaven that, if the reduction took place, we would annihilate the system and cause the day of reckoning. I then
35   addressed a meeting of 12,000. I later went to Stalybridge and

addressed a meeting of 10,000. I then addressed a meeting at Hyde of
10,000 and at Dukinfield of 5,000. At every meeting they came to a
resolution to work no more till they got the same wages as they had
in February 1840. . . . In the course of the last three weeks I have
40 addressed upwards of 300,000 in different parts of Lancashire and
Cheshire. We then went to Droylsden and Manchester, and the
people of Droylsden swore by the God of Heaven they would not
work any more until they had got their price of 1840. They then
came to Stockport and caused all mills to be stopped. . . .
45 You must be sure and stick out, and not go to your work; for if
you do the masters will crush you down. . . . I know the law of
conspiracy and there never was a good thing got, but some one had
to suffer for it. But they may put me in prison for I don't care a damn
for being within the prison walls. . . .

> Report of a speech by Richard Pilling at Stockport, 15 August
> 1842, reported by a constable, mentioned at his trial, and
> quoted in Jenkins, op cit, pp 120–1

Questions

a Explain 'lumpers' (line 1) and 'bellman' (line 32).
b Discuss Pilling's attack on the Government (lines 13–15).
c Was Pilling an effective leader by his own account? Which parts
   of his speeches would have made him so?
d Comment on the importance of education in many Chartist
   speeches. How much elementary education was there by the
   early 1840s?

9   The Voice of the Millowners?

Our columns are filled with particulars of the strangest and wildest
Holiday-Insurrection that has ever been attempted; an *Insurrection*
conducted in the name of *'peace, law, and order!'* – an Insurrection, yet
in some respects the most harmless, known in the modern history of
5 England: – an Insurrection more foolish than wicked in the dupes
who have caught the contagion, but we fear much more wicked than
foolish in the leaders who planned it. . . .
  If any class is so deplorably ignorant as to imagine that they are
observing *Law and Order* whilst they are ranging the country,
10 forcibly putting a stop to industry, crippling the first movement of
every mill and every workshop, driving the workmen from their
labour, and preventing the masters from making use of their own
lawful property, – and all this for the avowed purpose of *overawing
the Government*, and compelling it to change the Constitution; – if,
15 we say, any class is so deplorably ignorant as to think that acts like
these are justifiable, are honest, are consistent with the existence of
Freedom or of Peace; – if they think that the Terror inspired, the

Tyranny exercised, and the immense Danger incurred, may be
excused because the authors of these acts do not commit wholesale
20 destruction, rapine, and bloodshed; – however we may commiserate
such ignorance, it is necessary for every friend of his country to
exclaim with a voice of earnest warning and indignant reprehension,
that LAW AND ORDER MUST BE MAINTAINED. . . .

Our conviction is that the real cause of the present Insurrection is
25 long-continued, wide-spread, gnawing Distress, which we commiserate with our whole hearts; and which we have strenuously
laboured to prevent or to cure: but by the destruction of Law and
Order that Distress will be *immensely aggravated*. . . .

> 'The Holiday-Insurrection', editorial of Edward Baines,
> *Leeds Mercury*, 20 August 1842, quoted in Royle, op cit, pp
> 105–6

Questions

a What was the significance of the phrase *'Holiday-Insurrection'* (line
   2)?
b In condemning the events of August 1842 did Baines offer
   feasible alternatives to the methods used by the Chartists?
c Compare Baines's analysis in lines 24–5 with those of Carlyle in
   Chapter IV, document 11.
d *'Law and Order must be maintained'* (line 23). Was this why the
   'Plug Plot' / General Strike of 1842 had to be defeated, whatever
   the merits of its case?

VI Attitude, Alliance and Acrimony? – Chartism and the Middle Class

By 1840 Chartism was already clearly divided into various factions – what contemporaries called 'parties' – each with their own view of how to achieve the People's Charter. Though physical-force Chartism still had its place it had been devalued by the failure of the first petition in 1839 and the mass arrests following the Birmingham Convention. Scottish Chartists and the London Chartists of the LWMA were to move in the direction of self-help. Christian Chartism, Teetotal Chartism, Lovett's New Move, all implied that the working man must reach certain moral, religious or educational standards before the vote could be obtained. To O'Connor this was betrayal, a withdrawal from class conflict, a move in the direction of class co-operation.

In 1842 his fears were borne out in the attempts to achieve class co-operation in the form of the Complete Suffrage Union. Engels and Marx argued that Chartism was a class movement, but Lovett was not alone in seeing Chartism as a national movement in which the middle class had as much right to take part as the working class. Both classes shared common hostilities towards the aristocracy, though as the opening sections show they were suspicious of each other's motives. Had the middle class not betrayed the working class in 1832? Did they not oppose factory reform? Patricia Hollis is correct when she states that: 'Co-operation with the middle class was something of a tactical and intellectual tightrope'. Lovett was patently aware of this. He knew that O'Connor would use any sign of concession as a weapon to help his struggle for supremacy within the Chartist movement. Alliance turned on the Charter. Only total support by the middle class for the Charter would be acceptable. Only then would alliance be possible.

It was, however, on the motives for alliance that discussions broke down. For Lovett the Charter was not negotiable even though at the April 1842 conference discussion on it was delayed. The working class wanted the Charter now. The middle class saw the Charter as an end to be achieved at some future date. Sturge saw alliance as a means of obtaining better class relations and reducing tensions, a positive attempt to use religious belief to create a better society. But his idealism was out of step with much middle-class thinking. Repeal of the Corn Laws and Household Suffrage rather than Universal Suffrage were what practical men called for. To them an alliance with the working class was a lever, as it had been in 1832. In the end all the negotiations in 1842 succeeded in doing was to bring Lovett and O'Connor together (albeit briefly). To Chartists in general it reinforced their belief that the middle class was quite willing to take but only disposed to concede so much, and that insufficient.

1 Working-class Views of the Middle Class

(a) Gammage's view

The middle class, finding themselves not sufficiently powerful alone, had invoked the aid of the labouring millions, and the two classes combined made every available spot echo and re-echo with the now popular cry of reform. The press began to teem with the
5 speeches and articles urging the justice and necessity of a more extended system of representation, and to back the loud demand, Captain Swing assumed his authority in several large and important towns; and although some of the agents of this destructive warfare suffered the penalty of their transgressions, these proceedings only
10 hastened the coming empire of the middle class . . . the Reform Act, after repeated rejections, passed both Houses and received the royal assent. Thus was established the Charter of the middle class. The aristocracy had availed themselves of the aid of that class to crush Democracy, little dreaming that they were contracting obligations
15 to a power which would ultimately crush themselves. . . . The middle class persuaded them [the working class] for a season to forgo their more extensive claims, in order the more effectually to secure them ultimately. . . . This was the promise invariably held out to the working class whenever they ventured to moot the broader question
20 of popular sovereignty.
R. C. Gammage, op cit, pp 2–3

Questions

a Explain the reference to Captain Swing (line 7). How accurate is Gammage's conclusion about Swing's role in the achievement of reform in 1832?
b In what ways did 1832 establish 'the Charter of the middle class' (line 12)?
* c Gammage divided society into aristocracy, middle class and working class. In what ways is this too simplistic an explanation of society in the 1830s?
d Is Gammage accurate in stating that 'The aristocracy had availed . . . to a power which would ultimately crush themselves' (lines 12–15)?

e Was the working population in the 1830s as naïve as Gammage makes out?

(b) Engels

... Since the working-men do not respect the law, but simply submit to its power when they cannot change it, it is most natural that they should at least propose alterations in it, that they should wish to put a proletarian law in the place of the legal fabric of the
5 bourgeoisie. ... Chartism was from the beginning in 1835 chiefly a movement among the working-men, though not yet sharply separated from the radical petty-bourgeoisie. The Radicalism of the workers went hand in hand with the Radicalism of the bourgeoisie; the Charter was the shibboleth of both. They held their National
10 Convention every year in common, seeming to be one party. ... [By 1840] the bourgeoisie turned its attention to more practical projects, more profitable for itself, namely the Corn Laws. The Anti-Corn Law Association was formed in Manchester, and the consequence was a relaxation of the tie between the Radical
15 bourgeoisie and the proletariat. The working-men soon perceived that for them the abolition of the Corn Laws could be of little use, while very advantageous to the bourgeoisie. ... The fruit of the uprising [the Plug Plots] was the decisive separation of the proletariat from the bourgeoisie. The Chartists had not hitherto
20 concealed their determination to carry the Charter at all costs, even that of revolution; the bourgeoisie, which now perceived, all at once, the danger with which any violent change threatened their position, refused to hear anything further of physical force ... the difference between Chartist democracy and all previous political bourgeois
25 democracy. Chartism is of an essentially social nature, a class movement. ...

> F. Engels, *The Condition of the Working Class in England in 1844*, E. Hobsbawm (ed) (Panther, 1972), pp 254–5, 259

Questions

a What explanation does Engels give for the break-up of the alliance between the 'Radicalism of the workers ... [and] the Radicalism of the bourgeoisie'?

b Why are the middle class according to Engels more concerned with concessions from the aristocracy than with a revolution?

c Engels emphasised the importance of the economic in understanding class and class relations. Does this lead him to reach conclusions about the relationship between the middle and working classes?

d Why was the issue of the Corn Laws not entirely an economic issue?

*   *e*   Why is Marx's perspective on industrialisation and social change so important for the historian?

(c) Criticism of the middle class

. . . The Bolton Free Press does us but justice, in intimating that THE CHARTER has not hitherto held up the middle classes to 'public odium', nor 'pandered to the prejudices of the working men', by an unmeasured vituperation of those above them in the scale of society.
5   We could not close our eyes to the sordid selfishness by which the middle class is characterised, but we did hope that the crushing despotism of the aristocracy, of which they as well as the working men are the victims, would, in due time, awaken them to a sense of their own real interests, and induce them to join working men
10   against the common enemy of both. Recent events have satisfied us that this hope is fallacious. For however hostile may be the interests of the aristocracy to the interests of the rest of society, the most bitter and virulent enemies of the labouring class are found amongst the middle classes. . . . By whom have the peaceable meetings of the
15   working men been dispersed by brute force? And at whose instigation have the hundreds of victims who now occupy felons' dungeons. . . ? The answer is, the middle classes – the 'respectable' tradesman – the 'shopocracy'. It is by these that the government has been incited to make war upon the Chartists; these are the men who,
20   even upon the threshold of the jury-box, have avowed to see 'all the Chartists hung'. . . . Repeal of the Corn Laws – Extension of the Suffrage – Vote by Ballot – Repeal of the Rate-Paying clause in the Reform Bill – inquiry into the alleged grievances and sufferings of the people – reduction of the pension list – and fifty other measures
25   intended to affect beneficially the interests of the masses, have been opposed and rejected, not by the representatives of the aristocracy, but by the representatives of the middle class. . . .

> *The Charter*, 17 November 1839; printed in an extended version in F. C. Mather (ed), *Chartism and Society*, 1980, pp 199–202

Questions

a   What criticisms does the Charter make of the middle class?
b   What do you understand by 'guilt by association'? How successful is this article in making the case against the middle class using guilt by association?
c   How valid are the criticisms of middle-class attitudes to the Poor Law?
*   *d*   Just how influential was the middle class in the reforms introduced by the Whigs between 1833 and 1841? Did they prevent 'measures intended to affect beneficially the interests of the masses'?

2 Middle-class Views of Chartism

(a) Harriet Martineau

And what are those stirrings? What was it all about? The difficulty of understanding and telling a story is from its comprehending so vast a variety of things and persons. Those who have not looked into Chartism think that it means one thing – a revolution. Some who
5 talk as if they assumed to understand it, explain that Chartism is of two kinds – Physical Force Chartism, and Moral Force Chartism – as if these were not merely an intimation of two ways of pursuing an object not yet described. Those who look deeper – who go out upon the moors by torchlight, who talk with a suffering brother under the
10 hedge, or beside the loom, who listen to the groups outside the Union workhouse, or in the public house among the Durham coal-pits, will feel long bewildered as to what Chartism is, and will conclude at last that it is another name for popular discontent – a comprehensive general term under which are included all protests
15 against social suffering. . . .

> H. Martineau, *History of England during the Thirty Years Peace*, 1849 vol II, pp 262–3; printed in P. Hollis (ed), op cit, p 215

(b) Archibald Alison

The working-classes have now proved themselves unworthy of that extension of the Suffrage for which they contend; and that, whatever doubts might formerly have existed on the subject in the minds of well-meaning and enthusiastic, but simple and ill-informed men, it is
5 now established beyond all doubt, that Universal Suffrage in reality means nothing else but universal pillage. . . . What the working-classes understand by political power, is just the means of putting their hands in their neighbours' pockets; and that it was the belief that the Reform Bill would give them that power, which was the
10 main cause of the enthusiasm in its favour, and the disgust of the failure of these hopes, the principal reason for the present clamour for an extension of the Suffrage. . . .

> A. Alison, 'The Chartists and Universal Suffrage', *Blackwood's Edinburgh Magazine*, September 1839; printed in ibid, pp 215–16

Questions

a How does Harriet Martineau demonstrate the diversity of Chartism? Is she correct in seeing it as a 'protest against human suffering'?

b How does Archibald Alison question the motives of Chartists?

c Middle-class views of Chartism tended to fall into two basic types. The first, often grounded in lack of understanding, based

itself upon fear of success by the Chartists. The second saw
Chartism as a term embracing all the social evils affecting the
labouring population. How do these two documents demonstrate these basic types? What devices do they use to make their
cases?

* d Did the middle class really understand the Chartist movement
and its aspirations?

(c) Macaulay's speech on the Charter 5 May 1842

. . . I have no more unkind feeling towards these petitioners than I
have towards the sick man, who calls for a draught of cold water,
although he is satisfied that it would be the death for him . . . but I
would not in the one case give the draught of water . . . because I
5 know that by doing so I shall only make a scarcity a famine, and by
giving such relief enormously increase the evil. No one can say that
such a spoilation of property as these petitioners point to would be to
the relief of the evils of which they complain, and I believe that no
one will deny, that it would be a great addition to the mischief which
10 is proposed to be removed. . . . Let us, if we can, picture to ourselves
the consequences of such a spoilation as it is proposed should take
place. Would it end with one spoilation? How could it? That distress
which is the motive now for calling on this House to interfere would
be only doubled and trebled by the act; the measures of distress
15 would become greater after that spoilation, and the bulwarks by
which fresh acts of the same character would have been
removed. . . . A great community of human beings – a vast people
would be called into existence in a new position; there would be a
depression, if not an utter stoppage, of trade, and of all those vast
20 engagements of the country by which our people were supported,
and how is it possible to doubt that famine and pestilence would
come along to wind up the effects of such a system.

Hansard 3/LXXX/49–52 printed in G. M. Young and W. D.
Handcock (eds), *English Historical Documents*, vol XII(i)
1833–1874 (London, 1956), pp 449–51

Questions

a Macaulay bases his argument upon the need to preserve
property. Discuss.
b How does Macaulay build up his case for the destructive results
of the Petition's aims? How effective is his speech as a piece of
oratory?
c For Macaulay and the middle class economic considerations were
always more important than political ones. Discuss.

3 Appeals to the middle class

(a) *Threat or promise?*

Gentlemen: – We address you in the language of brotherhood probably for the last time. Up to the very last moment you have shut your senses to reason: but now that the last moment for moral appeal has arrived, perhaps you will listen to this last appeal of the people.

5   With a folly that will be the wonder of future ages, you have placed a blind confidence in the Whig Aristocracy: you have surrendered into their hands your 'right of thought', and any decree they please to send forth you look upon it as if it were a decree from On High. . . .

Are you and your prosperity mortgaged to pay the borough-
10   mongers' debt? Are you not compelled to pay on an average three times the value for bread, meat, wine, spirits, tea and everything you consume, in order to support the Jew swindlers and a perfumed, insolent Aristocracy? . . . Is not the money plundered from the people and spent in the debauch of the Court or the profligacy of the
15   Continent; is the money, we ask, not virtually abstracted from your trade and profits? Would we carry our money away to squander it on the dancers, gamesters and prostitutes of the continental cities, or would we lay it out at home in food, clothing and other necessary articles, to the great benefit of domestic trade and manufacturers?
20   We entreat you, not for our sakes, but for *your own*, not for the sakes of our families, but for *your own wives and children*, to take up these questions like men, and calmly and rationally discuss their truth or falsehood. . . . If you are not blind, as hardened of heart as ever Pharoah was of old, you must perceive that a mighty, a
25   thorough, a radical change must now very speedily take place in the constitution of society in these islands, a change which it is not in your power to avert, though it is in your power to give it a peaceful character. . . .

And what will be the result of that strike of blood, which you
30   alone can avert? If successful, the people will look on their fallen brothers and apostrophise their mangled remains thus: 'Well, you were sacrificed by the middle classes; they could have saved you but they would not; they assisted and encouraged the aristocracy to murder you! Let desolation dwell in the homes that made your
35   homes desolate!' Middle classes: vengeance swift and terrible will then overtake you. . . .

> 'To the Middle Classes of the North of England', a placard printed in the *Northern Liberator*, 21 July 1839 and printed in full in D. Thompson (ed), *The Early Chartists*, 1971, pp 131–4

Questions

a   To what aspects of middle-class consciousness did this document appeal?

b Did the middle class ever place 'a blind confidence in the Whig Aristocracy'?

c What was the importance of lines 9–12 to the middle class and their opposition to the aristocracy?

d Do you think an appeal couched in this form would have its intended result? Why?

(b) Land v. industry – a means of appeal?

. . . Never, never will the bread tax be taken off as long as the House of Commons continues to be a parlour full of country squires, and that obsolete feudalism, the House of Lords, is suffered to control the will of the nation. For the repeal of the Corn Laws not a working
5 man throughout England or Scotland will move a muscle – for THE PEOPLE'S CHARTER there are at least two millions ready to hazard their lives. Are you, then, galloping on to ruin, Ye Master Manufacturers? Are you goaded down the steep by the tyrant agriculturalists: Hoist then the banner of the People's Charter! Cease
10 to cry to the landlords for corn. Seize the sickle of Universal Suffrage, that will cut it bravely. Our cause is, in reality, the same; if you mean fairly, our interests ought to be identical. Without your capital our labour is less available; without our labour your capital is useless. We are united by a bond of interest; but these lazy drones,
15 these vermin-breeding squires *they* are of use to no-one – they are a dead weight upon the kingdom – an incubus upon the industry of the earth. If they were every one of them swept away tomorrow, the nation would know it only by feeling herself lightened of a heavy weight. Why then should we by being divided suffer them to rule us
20 both – to starve us and ruin you? . . .
The Chartist, 23 February 1839

Questions

a Why do you think that the working-class appeal to the anti-agricultural feeling of the middle class had such force in 1839?

b The appeal takes an extreme form in its condemnation of the feudalism of land. How valid was this appeal?

c The working class saw political reform preceding economic reform in their appeals. Why?

* *d* Discuss the proposition that the fundamental difference between the middle class and working class in the 1830s and 1840s was that the former was a 'class of interests' and the latter a 'class of principles'.

(c) Robert Lowery's speech to a Leeds Parliamentary Reform Association meeting, January 1841

. . . Now, gentlemen, what do I, and all who are of my class say to

you – I use no menace to you; but I say it to you as a fact that you and I must sink together, and if we sink, you sink also along with us (*hear, hear*). I have wished for the day in which you would come to discuss
5   grievances with us, and to seek for a remedy. . . . I say no representation short of that which admits every man arrived at a mature age to a vote – that is to say Universal Suffrage (*hear, hear*). Why then talk to me about expediency. If expediency is right, then Universal Suffrage is right; and any thing short of Universal
10   Suffrage is not expedient. . . . It was found expedient to sacrifice the 40s. freeholders (*hisses and cheers*). It was found expedient to give up the principles of civil and religious liberty (*hisses and cheers*). And what is this of which we are complaining? Are we not here to complain of Lord Melbourne's government? Are you Whigs
15   satisfied with it, or are you not? (*hisses and cheers*). . . . The Whigs are men of expediency and they have ruined their own cause by it. . . . They have taught us a lesson, and we know from them, that he who trusts to expediency, trusts to a broken stick (*hear, hear*). Then what Suffrage should we have? should it be an individual's right or should
20   it be property? The individual right is the only test of the Suffrage for the people. Every man amenable to the law has the right to be a maker of the laws. When you get Universal Suffrage, you get all the intelligence of the nation; and by Household Suffrage you shut out a large portion of the intelligence of the people. It has never been
25   denied even by the most rabid Tory. They have always said that you have the right, but you are not wise enough to exercise it. Now, I ask you – have you not admitted in your own churches and chapels young persons of fifteen years of age to choose their own ministers and their own communions? Why? it is because they are old enough;
30   and then if they are wise enough to choose their own religion, surely they are wise enough to choose their own members of Parliament. . . .

B. Harrison and P. Hollis (eds), op cit, pp 253–5

Questions

a   What was the basis of Lowery's argument for Universal Suffrage? Why should the middle class accept it?
b   What was the difference between Universal and Household Suffrage and why was it so important in the working- and middle-class debate?
c   What was the main difference between Whig and Tory attitudes to the suffrage question according to Lowery? Account for these differences in attitude.
d   What does Lowery mean when he talks of the Whigs pursuing policies of expediency? Is he right in his criticisms?
*   e   Lowery's arguments may be logical and his conclusions fair *but* it did not succeed. Why?

4 1842 – the Year of Class-union?

This section will examine the attempts made to forge a union between the working and middle classes by the Complete Suffrage League. A study of the suffrage movement from a broader chronological framework is to be found in P. Hollis (ed), *Pressure from Without* (Edward Arnold, 1974).

The necessity for suffrage

(a) . . . Treat men as slaves, and they will soon betake themselves to the vices of slavery – would you fit them for freedom, you must make them free. . . . Tell any class of men that they are a worthless caste, not to be trusted with their own rights, incapable of
5   understanding their own wants – but a scant degree above the level of brutes – treat them with suspicion, call them the unwashed rabble, harass them with trespass and game laws, set before them the ultimate prospect of union-house fare and union-house confine-ment, and if you do not make them reckless and dissolute, careless
10 of others' rights, negligent of education and negligent of religion, it is no fault of yours. You have done your best. . . . On the whole, we have no manner of doubt that the moral effects to be anticipated from complete suffrage would be even more valuable than those which are purely political. The bonds by which society is held
15 together would be drawn more closely together – party conflicts would soon cease – reason and right would have fair play – education would be coveted – morals would improve – and religion itself would appeal with much greater probability of success to the myriads who now suspect it to be an instrument of oppression. . . .

> Nonconformist, 10 November 1841; printed in P. Hollis (ed),
> *Class and Conflict in Nineteenth Century England 1815–1850*,
> 1973, pp 273–4

(b) Deeply impressed with convictions of the evils arising from class legislation, and of the sufferings thereby inflicted upon our industri-ous fellow-subjects, the undersigned affirm that a large majority of the people of this country are unjustly excluded from that fair, full
5   and free exercise of the legislative franchise to which they are entitled by the great principles of Christian equity, and also by the British Constitution, for 'no subject of England can be constrained to pay any aids or taxes . . . but such as are imposed by his own consent, or that of his representative in Parliament'.

> Sharman Crawford's motion presented on 28 August 1841 to
> the Anti-Corn Law League conference in Manchester, where
> it obtained forty-one votes. It is printed in P. Hollis (ed),
> *Pressure from Without*, 1974, p 84

Questions

a   In what ways does document (a) show that the working class was not trusted?

b   What do the documents see the end product of complete suffrage as being? What view of society does this entail?

c   To both the Nonconformist and Crawford religion and politics were inseparable. How did this make inevitable the failure of class union?

*   *d*   To the middle-class radicals anti-slavery and complete suffrage were viewed in the same way. The problem was that in fact they were not the same. Discuss.

The Complete Suffrage League

(c) The Crown and Anchor Meeting January 1842
In January 1842, Mr Joseph Sturge, whose benevolent labours in the cause of humanity and freedom are so notorious, commenced his exertions in favour of what was called 'Complete Suffrage.' His first
5   effort was the preparing of a Memorial to the Queen . . . [to] promote in Parliament that full, fair and free representation of the people in the House of Commons to which they were entitled. . . . This Memorial having been sent to our Association for signature, it was resolved to give it all the support in our power; although, at the
10   same time, we felt bound to express our opinion, that neither a full nor fair representation of the people could be obtained till the essentials of the People's Charter were enacted as the laws of the realm. Soon after this, being at a Public Meeting at the Crown and Anchor, on the suffrage question, I was invited, with Messrs.
15   Hetherington, Parry and others to meet some of Mr. Sturge's friends in the refreshment room, to talk over the subject. After some very excellent speeches, there given, by Mr. Miall, Mr. Crawford, Mr. Spencer and others, Mr. George Thompson, the chairman, called upon me for my opinion. I told them that my definition of Complete
20   Suffrage was found in the People's Charter; all the principles of which I thought to be essential to secure the just representation of the people. . . .

      William Lovett, *Life and Struggles* . . . , op cit, pp 279–80

(d) The Birmingham Conference April 1842
. . . Shortly after this meeting I received a letter from Mr. Sturge, informing me that a Provisional Committee had been formed at Birmingham, and that they intended to call a Complete Suffrage Conference on 5th of April 1842.
5   This conference, composed of eighty-four persons, both of the middle and working classes – appointed for the most part by those who had signed the Memorial referred to – met at Birmingham at the

time specified. Mr. J. H. Parry and myself were appointed by the
members of our Association to attend it, and Mr. C. H. Neesom and
Mr. Charles Westerton, two other of our members, were also
delegated. . . . The members of our Association, conceiving that
there was little chance of a cordial union being effected between the
two classes without the recognition of the Charter . . . were anxious
to bring this document forward as one of the first subjects for
discussion. But the Business Committee objecting to this course, the
consideration of it was delayed till other matters had been discussed.
These were the essential principles that were thought to be requisite
for securing a full, fair and free representation of the people; these
were accordingly discussed, and after a very long and earnest debate,
we were gratified in seeing most of the principles of our Charter
adopted. On the third day, therefore, according to the arrangements
previously agreed on, I brought forward the following motion:–
  'That this Conference having adopted such just principles of
representation as are necessary for giving to all classes of society their
equal share of political power, and as the People's Charter contains
such details as have been deemed necessary for the working out of
such principles, and has, moreover, been adopted by millions of our
brethren as the embodiment of their political rights, this Conference,
in order to effect a cordial union of the middle and working classes,
resolve in *a future conference* (in which the working classes may be
more fully represented) to enter into a calm consideration of that
document amongst plans of political reform, and, if approved of, to
use every just and peaceable means for creating a public opinion in its
favour.'
  In the lengthened discussion which arose on this resolution, it
appeared that considerable prejudice existed in the minds of many of
the middle class members against the Charter; though the resolution
did not call upon them to agree to that document, but only to take it
into consideration. . . . However, to conciliate feeling against us,
without any deviation of principle, we Chartists eventually modified
the resolution as follows, fully believing that the majority would not
oppose a fair discussion of the Charter at the next conference. . . .
This having been adopted, and the rules for the formation of a new
society entitled 'The National Complete Suffrage Union'; and, after
some few other business resolutions, concluded its sittings, it having
lasted four days.
  This effort to effect a union between the two classes was to some
extent successful; for a great many local Complete Suffrage Associations were formed in many towns. Great numbers of the working
classes were however, kept aloof from it, by the abuse and
misrepresentation of the *Northern Star*; and others who, so far,
approved of the principles of the Union, were not disposed to forego
their own agitation for the Charter to join it till they had tested it by
another conference. In the meantime, however, the members of the

55   Union were not idle; tracts were printed, lectures given, meetings held and, to the best of my recollection, two motions introduced into the House of Commons on the subject of the Suffrage by Mr. Sharman Crawford.
          Ibid, pp 280–2

(e) . . . It was with no ordinary satisfaction that Bainbridge and myself, with the best of his mates and colleagues hailed this new movement (Complete Suffrage) . . . when Joseph Sturge and his friends, a little later, resolved to hold a conference in Birmingham, to
5   which all the Chartist Associations were invited to send delegates, I joined with the Yeovil Chartists in labouring to promote it . . . early in April 1842 I set out joyfully for Birmingham, where I was most cordially welcomed. William Lovett, John Collins and their adherents, came in considerable force, though in some 'fear and trembl-
10   ing', lest they should be entrapped into any compromises or concessions that might ruin their characters with those who had delegated them, even if the Chartist movement itself was not otherwise injured. But fortunately Feargus O'Connor, and therefore his party, stood aloof, not choosing to accept any offers, or a share in
15   the leadership of any movement, which would commit them to an alliance with middle-class and moderate-minded men like Sturge and his friends. . . . The only minister of religion, besides myself, to attend was the Rev. Thos. Spencer M.A. . . . .
      But while . . . Sturge, Miall, Sharman Crawford . . . and other
20   middle class supporters of 'Complete Suffrage' met the Chartists and conferred with them just as frankly and honestly as Lovett and his friends met themselves, a painful feeling was at first excited among the Chartists when they found that a well-to-do young Quaker 'Cotton-Lord' had come from Rochdale to take part in the Confer-
25   ence as a friend of Mr. Sturge. . . . It was John Bright who had thus descended upon us. . . . Hence the Chartist delegates were as much surprised as gratified to find that not only Mr Sturge . . . but even this sturdy Rochdale capitalist, were willing to meet them and their demands in a friendly and conciliatory spirit. Yet how much depends
30   in such cases on the character of the leaders. With Sturge at the head of one side and Lovett on the other, it was not wonderful that mutual confidence was speedily established, difficulties were smoothed away, concessions, where necessary, made (chiefly, I admit, by the Sturge party). . . . On the fourth and final day the last of the six
35   points of the People's charter was to be discussed – Annual Parliaments – and to this I believe, all of Sturge's friends, including myself, naturally had a strong objection . . . but they (the Chartists) knew that if they consented to have even this comparatively unimportant point removed from their Charter, and replaced by
40   'triennial Parliaments' the whole of the O'Connor party . . . would at once declare that they had betrayed the Chartist cause. . . . While if

they refused compliance, and thereby alienated their new and influential friends, they would be nullifying the whole labours and results of the Conference. . . . It must have been a terribly anxious
45 time for them, that Thursday night and Friday morning. They represented the matter forcibly to Sturge and the rest of us; some of them admitting that the difference between Annual and Triennial Parliaments was far too trifling to compensate for the serious evils which insistence on it would cause, but pleading for one more
50 concession to save their political lives . . . it was announced on the last day of the Conference that the 'Complete Suffrage' friends had agreed to waive their objections to placing Annual Parliaments in the programme for future discussion. . . .

Henry Solly, *'These Eighty Years' or The Story of an Unfinished Life* (London, 1893), vol I, pp 176–9

Questions

a   In what ways do the two accounts of the Birmingham conference differ? Why do you think that these differences occurred?
b   Using the three documents, write a narrative account of events in the movement for Complete Suffrage between January and April 1842.
c   On what issues did the working–class and middle–class delegates disagree at Birmingham? How successfully were these disagreements resolved?
d   What was the attitude of O'Connor? Why was this difficult to understand for contemporaries?
*   e   For Complete Suffrage to succeed there would have to be compromise on both sides. But compromise alienated working–class and middle–class support. Does this explain the ultimate failure of Complete Suffrage?

(g) Interlude
. . . In September 1842, a special meeting of the Council of the Union was called at Birmingham to arrange, among other matters, for the calling of the next conference. Now as O'Connor (notwithstanding his hostility to the Union) had boasted largely of his intention to get
5 the working classes fully represented in the next conference, if he spent half he possessed – which in reality meant that he would get it packed with his own disciples, if possible – it became a question, with those who wanted a fair conference of both classes chosen, how it could best be prevented. In talking the matter over with my
10 friends, I suggested that this could be best done by one-half of the representatives being chosen by the electors, and half by non-electors; and that if they interfered with each other's meetings the election should be void. . . . The Complete Suffrage party, however, instead of defending it as a fair and just mode of choosing a

15   deliberative assembly . . . foolishly gave way on this very important
point at almost their first meeting they attended after its publication.
The result was that O'Connor immediately set about securing a
majority in the conference, recommending as candidates those of his
own party to every town where he thought their election could be
20   secured. The middle classes . . . finding that they were likely to be
outnumbered by the O'Connorites, and being, moreover, pre-
judiced against the charter, adopted a plan by which they thought to
get rid of Feargus and his party without ultimate injury to their
union. They, therefore, got two legal gentlemen in London, to
25   prepare a bill, founded on the principles they had adopted, and which
they designated 'The New Bill of Rights'. . . . I then expressed to Mr.
Sturge my great regret at this course of proceeding, as I thought that
the putting forth of this measure in opposition to the charter would
destroy all chances of union between the two classes, as myself and
30   others who had joined them could not with any consistency vote for
their 'Bill of Rights' in opposition to the charter, and that I believed
that the majority of the working classes would not desert the
document they had so long fought for, for this new measure the
council had prepared. . . .

W. Lovett, op cit, pp 282, 288–9

(h)   The December conference

Leicester was privileged to return four delegates. The Complete
Suffrage party wished two of the delegates to be chosen in a meeting
composed of parliamentary electors only; and to leave the unrepre-
sented to elect the two other delegates. But this did not meet the
5   views either of Chartists or of working men generally. They forced
their way into the meetings called by the respectables; and the
respectables disappeared. It was of their own respectable good
pleasure that they withdrew. If they had remained, working men
would have voted for the Rev. J. P. Mursell and Mr. William Baines,
10   to be delegates with Duffy and myself. . . . So we acted by ourselves.
I and Duffy and two other Chartists were voted delegates for
Leicester, and we went to Birmingham: no respectables went.

Our Chartist delegates were the most numerous party in the
Birmingham Conference; but my expectation rose when I saw so
15   many persons present belonging to the middle class. . . . But there
was no attempt to bring about a union – no effort for conciliation –
no generous offer of the right hand of friendship. We soon found that
it was determined to keep poor Chartists 'at arm's length'. We were
not to come between the wind and *their* nobility. Thomas Beggs of
20   Nottingham, a mere secondary member of the Complete Suffrage
party, was put up to propose their first resolution – That the
'People's Bill of Rights' form the basis from which the petition
should be drawn that this Conference would present to Parliament.
. . . Murmurs of discontent and soon of indignation began to arise

25   – when up rose William Lovett and. . . to our utter amazement he led
the attack upon them. If they had made up their minds, he said, to
force their Bill of Rights upon the Conference, he would move that
the People's Charter be the basis from whence the petition should be
drawn for presentation to Parliament. . . . We had looked on Lovett
30   and his friends as a doubtful party when the Conference was opened.
All thought of that was now gone; and the debate soon began to be
very stormy – for the Complete Suffrage party stuck by their
'People's Bill of Rights' and we stuck by our People's Charter. . . .
When the decisive vote was taken, we were apparently as three to
35   one; and Joseph Sturge, after a little hesitation, rose and told us that
he and his friends had come to the determination to leave us: they
would withdraw and hold a Conference by themselves. All was
tumult for a time. An independent Quaker, from the Isle of Wight,
protested, and said he would not withdraw. The Rev. H. Solly of
40   Yeovil also refused to withdraw. . . . Henry Vincent, with his
characteristic modesty . . . and with his proverbial attachment to
respectability, withdrew with the Complete Suffrage party.

        T. Cooper, *The Life of Thomas Cooper*, 1872, J. Saville (ed)
        (Leicester, 1971), pp 220–7

(i) This second conference, consisting of 374 members, met in
Birmingham on Tuesday Dec. 27th. 1842. . . . After some minor
business regarding the letters received, and the election of members,
they proceeded to consider the most important part of their
5   programme, this new bill. When, therefore, my friends Mr Thomas
Beggs and Mr John Dunlop had proposed the resolution. . . . I rose
to urge on the Complete Suffrage friends the necessity for withdraw-
ing that part of the resolution if union were to be maintained. I
endeavoured also to remind them, that I was induced to modify my
10   resolution regarding the charter at the last conference, on the
understanding that its details would be discussed at the present
one. . . . The next morning, they not being disposed to yield the
point regarding their bill, I proposed the following amendment,
which O'Connor seconded. . . . But I regret to say, that this
15   reasonable proposal was not acceded to, those gentlemen rather
wishing that the motion and amendment should go to the vote. The
vote being consequently taken, there appeared for the original
motion of Mr. Beggs 94 and for my amendment 193. After this
decision the minority left the conference and met in another place to
20   discuss their Bill; and the majority continued their sittings to discuss
the details of the Charter. . . .

        W. Lovett, op cit, pp 289–91

Questions

a How did the methods used to elect representatives reflect the differences between middle and working classes?

b In what ways was the December conference a victory for O'Connor and a defeat for Lovett?

c Using the extracts, produce a narrative of the main developments in the campaign for Complete Suffrage between September and December 1842.

d How far was the failure of Complete Suffrage a result of the middle class limiting their definition of 'respectability' to exclude many members of the working class?

* e Was union between the middle and working classes ever really likely in 1842?

Further work

a 1842 was the year of all-round defeat for the Chartists. Discuss.

b Examine the relationship between the Anti-Corn Law League and the Chartists between 1838 and 1846.

c Discuss the proposition that for the middle class in the 1840s reform was a moral question first, a political question second, whereas for the working class it was the other way round.

VII   The Chartist Land Plan

Introduction

'The people's right to the land, stolen from them at the Norman Conquest, had. . . long been a radical slogan' (C. Thorne). The Land Plan was very much O'Connor's scheme, and his book fully outlined his ideas. It was a curious amalgam, offering 'a mixture of the self-help of Smiles and the speculative attractions of Hudson' (ibid), seasoned with pinches of Robert Owen (New Lanark) and the mid-seventeenth-century Diggers led by Gerard Winstanley.

The Land Plan was enormously popular; announced in 1845, the National Land Company was established two years later, offering shares at £1.6.0. There were soon 70,000 members paying weekly subscriptions of £3,200 by May 1847 – including 620 members in Sheffield and 345 in Barnsley – enabling O'Connor to purchase five estates. Two of these, O'Connorville in Hertfordshire and Charterville in Oxfordshire, are featured in this section; the others were Snig's End and Lowbands in Gloucestershire and Dodford in Worcestershire.

Despite the optimism of the *Northern Star* in August 1846 that 'there is nothing the land will not do in the way of support and comfort' O'Connor faced much opposition: in June 1848 he told a meeting in Sheffield that 'every little editor, some of whom do not know whether potatoes are dug up ready to roast and buttered, or whether they grow upon trees, are all attacking my scheme'. But the same applied to many of the tenants, as the *Victoria County History* entry reports. All but two of the Charterville tenants soon left their house, stable and pigsty. It was ironic that most agricultural labourers would have prospered on these estates where town dwellers failed miserably.

O'Connor's enthusiasm kept the Company going until 1851 when a parliamentary Select Committee investigated it, and the Company was dissolved. The small houses and allotments still remain at Charterville between the old and new A40 at Minster Lovell; they are a reminder of how Chartism could look back as well as forward.

1 O'Connor's Scheme

The object which I have in view in submitting a practical work upon the management of small farms to the working men of this country is, that each man who is willing to work may be independent of every other man in the world for his daily bread; so that the prosperity of the country shall consist in an aggregate of happy individuals, rather than in a community of a few owners of all its aggregate wealth; and upon whose speculation, whim, and caprice, the poor man must now depend for his bread. If I was to allow myself to enter upon a political discussion, I think I should be enabled to convince all those who boast of a love of country, that, upon the cultivation of their own domestic resources alone must the wealth, the stability, and the happiness of a people depend:– that in all our commercial transactions foreign countries can interfere so as materially to disarrange those rules and regulations by which trade and traffic are governed; and that such interference materially affects the condition of the working classes; which our land, and that alone, is a branch of the national wealth with which no foreign state can by possibility interfere. England has long been the work-shop of the world; and while her sons were employed in the manufacture of that machinery by which their own labour has now become a drug, they had not the foresight to discover that they were violating even the Malthusian rule, by creating the very worst description of over-population, a surplus which had no power of resistance, no rights to contend for, and consumed nothing: a surplus of machinery. . . . I seek to open a field so wide that for centuries to come the people of this country would not be an overstock for the pasture. . . .

I declare it as my opinion that no Minister, that no party, that no combination of interests, can long withhold the land from its legitimate, most just, and most profitable uses. . . . It is almost an insult to the understanding of a working man to remind him, that as long as the vast estates of the present proprietors best serve the purposes of their owners by so leasing them in such large and unprofitable allotments as will give to the tenant an interest in the holding greater than as a free man he will have in his vote, and so long as the use of that vote by the landlord gives to him political patronage to a much larger amount than he has sacrificed by the mal-appropriation of his land, so long will the land be used by him as a mere political machine, and so long will the people, disinherited from the land, be looked upon as slaves living upon sufferance.

The question may here arise then, as to which of the changes that I contend for should have the priority:– the establishment of the small farm principle – or the enactment of the People's Charter, by which the land would be stripped of its political qualification. . . . I do not believe that any other inducement, save that of the practical result of the plan of small farms, ever will be sufficiently strong to produce

such a public feeling as will bring into moral action such an amount of mind in favour of both changes, as neither minister or party would dare to resist. Therefore . . . I incline to think that the possession of political power is indispensable as a means for making the plan of
50 free labour a national benefit. . . .

In conformity then with the terms of my belief, I am about to present to the industrious of all classes the means whereby social happiness, political freedom, and the pure spirit of religion, may be introduced . . . as a substitute for the misery, the discomfort, and the
55 immorality at present prevailing. . . .

Sixty persons subscribe eighty pounds in one year, which . . . is to be laid out in the purchase of four acres of ground, worth four pounds a-year for ever – only one person can become possessed of the land . . . [the] sixty subscribers go into a lottery, wherein there are
60 fifty-nine blanks and one prize, A gets the prize, and with it a lease for ever of four acres of ground, at four pounds a-year . . . after the fifty-nine blanks have been drawn, the fifty-nine persons drawing them go into another lottery, wherein there are eight prizes of ten shillings a-year for ever each, that is, the four pounds rent
65 conditioned to be paid by him who draws the land, is divided into eight shares of ten shillings each. . . .

The scale which I have laid down for the disposal of four acres would equally apply to four million acres, or any quantity of land. . . .
70 I feel convinced that a community consisting of one hundred men, occupying four acres each, would be a more contented body, a more industrious body, and a more united body, than a hundred individuals located upon the same four hundred acres, managed by the master minds of the whole body; while the community of self-acting
75 individuals would have the advantage of the superior knowledge and skill of the master minds of their body. I believe that in what is called the community-principle, improvement is likely to stop or flag at that point at which moderate comfort is insured. . . .

I look upon the experiments made by Mr. Owen for the
80 improvement of the physical condition of all classes of society, but more especially the working classes, as having far exceeded in utility those of any other individual who has ever lived before him. . . . I very much prefer the community-principle, as practised by Mr. Owen to the present system; while I very much prefer the
85 co-operative system, with individual responsibility and possession, to the community principle. . . .

Rules for the Practical Management of a Four Acre Farm.

I must shew what four acres are capable of producing by the labour of one man . . . Mr. Cobbett has placed beyond doubt . . . that
90 a quarter of an acre of ground of moderate quality is capable of supporting a cow throughout the year . . . that one cow will make a sufficiency of manure within the year for an acre of land and . . . one

man by sixteen days' labour will be able to support a cow from the produce of a quarter of an acre. . . .

95   The several crops, to the production of which four acres of land, with the labour of one man, may be most beneficially applied.

1 Acre of Potatoes

1 Acre of Wheat

1¾ Acres to be appropriated as hereinafter described – and

100   ¼ of an acre for kitchen garden.

The stock to be fed upon the produce of the land so cultivated to consist of –

4 Cows

6 Pigs

105   6 Sheep

Poultry

. . . In fact there is no reason why any other man could not make as much profit of four acres of land as I could make, and I undertake to

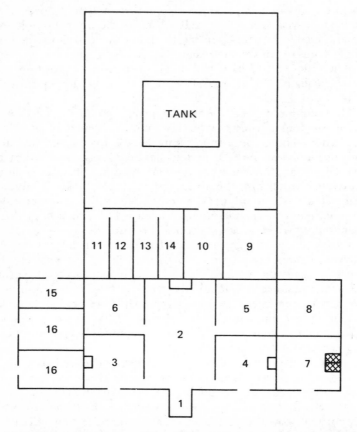

GROUND PLAN OF DWELLING HOUSE, OFFICES, AND FARM YARD

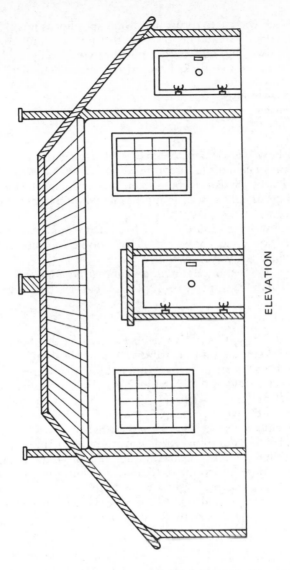

ELEVATION

test the success, by making two hundred pounds clear profit of four
110   acres of middling ground, over and above what shall be consumed
by an able-bodied man, his wife and family, besides housing them
well, and clothing them well, and not allowing them to want a single
comfort that a working man is entitled to, and ought to enjoy. . . .

One great object . . . and . . . the very next in importance to the
115   house for the family, is that of houses for the stock. I know full well
that a man possessed of four acres of ground, and who had to walk
some distance to his farm, would be very apt to throw up some kind

of a hovel wherein to thrust himself as speedily as possible. His first
care, therefore, should be to secure the means of building himself a
120 suitable dwelling, and as that purpose could only be effected by
profit made of his stock, I would recommend him to commence
with his out-offices . . . :–
 A Cow-House . . .
 Sheep-House . . .
125 Pig-Stye . . .
 Dairy . . .
The Fowl-House, and A Shed for Farming Implements, with a
sufficiency taken off for a commodious privy.
 All except the dairy should front the yard, and the dairy, for the
130 advantage of light as well as appearance, should be entered from the
front. . . .
 The Dwelling House . . . is forty feet long in the clear, and
nineteen feet wide, consisting of five rooms, and no stairs or back
door which is always a nuisance. . . .
 F. O'Connor, *A Practical Work on the Management of Small
Farms*, 1843, pp v, 10–12, 103–4, 114–15, 150–1, 159, 169–71

Questions

a What was O'Connor's reason for writing this book? Examine
   the Scheme's economic validity and implications.
b Discuss the statement that 'our land, and that alone, is a branch of
   the national wealth with which no foreign state can by possibility
   interfere' (lines 16–18).
c What are the reasons for O'Connor stressing the importance of
   the land, and especially of *small* farms?
d Explain in your own words how the Land Plan would work.
e Examine the farming techniques and the house suggested by
   O'Connor, and compare them with common rural practice in
   'the golden age of English agriculture'.
f What fundamental points did O'Connor apparently not consider, and how serious were they to be in the collapse of his
   scheme?

2 O'Connorville: the Problems

In 1846 Feargus O'Connor acquired Heronsgate, or Herringsgate,
near Chorley Wood, for £2,344 in the interest of the future National
Land Company. After 19 acres of coppice had been grubbed up for
arable the whole 103 acres were laid out for agriculture on
5 O'Connor's plan. The thirty-five allotments varied from 2 to 4 acres.
Thirty-five cottages were built; at first the 2-acre houses were built
with three rooms, the 3-acre houses with four . . .; each had a flagged
day-room with a bedroom on each side, a back kitchen, dairy,

cowhouse, henhouse and pigsty. They were well built. The school-
10 house built by the company had 2 acres of ground attached; in
addition, the master was paid by the parents. The cost of these
buildings and the clearing and manuring of the ground was about
£6,700.

The directors expected to 'reproduce' this sum by the profits of the
15 sales of the allotments, the prices of which would rise through the
labour put into the ground by the tenants. In the meantime the
tenants were to pay as rent 4 per cent. on the outlay, or £9 10s. 10d. on
a 3-acre holding. But after some had been settled for twelve months
the calculations necessary to fix the cottage-rents had not been
20 begun. The allotments were to be cultivated by hand labour.
Herringsgate, or O'Connorville, was fully settled in about a year. The
mistakes of the promoter were at once revealed. The men who came
to take up the holdings were small tradesmen, merchants or weavers
from the manufacturing towns. They understood the ground as little
25 as their wives understood the henhouse or dairy; they even had to
buy bread because they knew not how to bake. After nearly a year's
settlement they had made no provision of manure, except in so far as
a landowner allowed them to collect rotten leaves in the woods.
They put in their potato harvest, saying that they must take their
30 chance. They could not bear an out-of-door life and hired at 12s. a
week labourers to whom the farmers paid 8s. to 9s. The prospect for
the poor settlers was rather the workhouse than the idyllic home-
stead.

This mistake was a gross one, but the next was ironically near the
35 truth. The settlers were engaged to cultivate the land, by spade and
fork, for the same crops as farmers of 100 acres. Evidence taken
before the committee proved that vegetables were profitable on such
holdings. The proximity to London was another argument in favour
of what we should call French gardening or intensive culture. But it
40 was madness to put men who were not even labourers into
competition with farmers, spade work into competition with the
plough in arable farming, handwork into competition with the best
machinery. Moreover, Herringsgate was pasture land. What the
scheme represented in the country-side is shown by the attitude of
45 the labourers. They would have liked, they said, to try to make a
living on the holdings if they were able to plough. The cottages were
exactly what was needed in Hertfordshire. If the scheme had been
planned for the agricultural labourer, with greater experience of
farming, it might have been prosperous and beneficial. It repre-
50 sented, however, 'the townsman's dream of country life.'
Victoria County History of Hertfordshire, IV, 1914, pp 230–1

Questions

a How was O'Connorville to finance itself?

b   What mistakes were made in the planning of the community in
      (i) the size of holdings;
      (ii) the kind of farming;
      (iii) the choice of allotment holders?
c   Do you agree with the conclusion that communities such as this
      represented 'the townsman's dream of country life' (line 50)?
d   What attempts were made after the failure of the Land Plan to
      bring town and country together?

3   The Visual Evidence

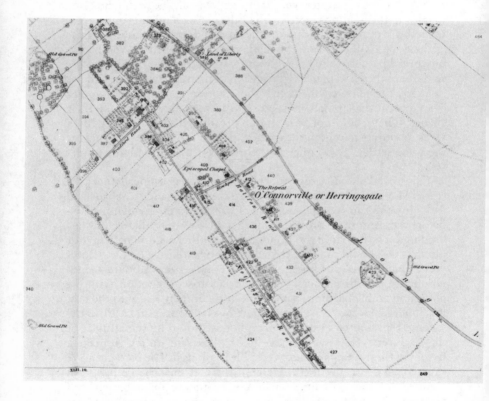

Questions

a   Identify the surviving features of the Chartist settlements on the
      two maps.
b   Why might the roads of O'Connorville have been named after
      certain towns?

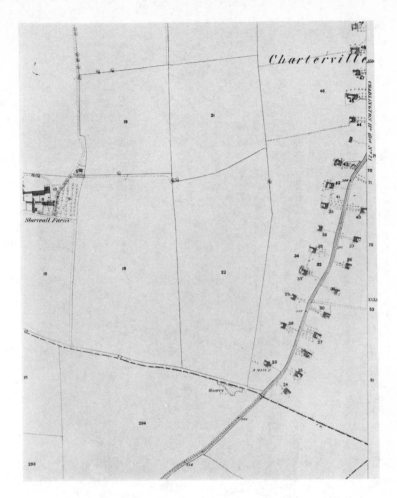

O'Connorville and Charterville Allotments from the 1:2500 1st
edition Ordnance Survey maps, Herts. 43/6 (1872) and Oxon. 31/6
(1880). NOT TO SCALE

c To what extent do the buildings and land boundaries agree with
   the dimensions in document 1?
d Compare the map and engraving of O'Connorville.
e Which features of the engraving suggest an idealised image of the
   settlement?
f Of what value are good-quality maps to the local historian?

The promise of a new life: O'Connorville

4 O'Connorville: a Chartist Arcadia?

On arriving at O'Connorville. . . . we had ocular demonstration that
this demonstration was no mere metropolitan excursion but 'A
National Jubilee' in favour of the 'Universal Rights' of man, each
county appearing to have at least a fair share of representatives
present. . . .

   On entering the gates, the band played 'The Chartist Land
March'. . . . a huge tri-coloured banner floating, high above an
immense chesnut tree, [bore] the inscription 'O'Connorville'; and
secondly, Rebecca, the Chartist Cow, like the Sacred Cows of old,
clothed in her vesture of tri-colour, rendered holy by the popular
voice, which is the voice of God; next the immense Dancing Booth
. . . attracting the attention of everyone. The remaining booths, for
refreshment and amusement, were also of a very elegant character. . . .

   About half-past twelve, coaches and four, coaches and pairs, gigs,
carts and wagons, began to arrive from all points, and shortly after
about two hundred vans, freighted with the sons of toil, began to
arrive, many of them bearing suitable banners. . . . The whole estate
was traversed, and for the first time in the world's history not one of
the vast multitude found a single fault, but outstripped each other in
encomiums, declaring that all was perfection. The thing that
appeared most to astonish, was the size of the allotments. Few would
believe that four acres was such a spacious tract of land. . . . Every
inch of it is capable of being turned into the richest garden ground in
a SINGLE SEASON. It will not take years to improve it; all it requires is
kindness. . . . The situation is heavenly, picturesque, and most
healthy, and to me it appears a perfect paradise. . . . I should dearly
love to have a home in the centre of every branch of my numerous
family. . . .

Your faithful friend and bailiff,

FEARGUS O'CONNOR

The *Northern Star*, 22 August 1846

The Land! The Land! The Land!

   Whit-Monday . . . presented to the eye of the agrarian reformer
indubitable proofs of the great, growing, and almost universal
interest felt not only by the masses who toil but by many who live by
the labour of others, in that great and noble work so well begun by
the Chartist Convention of 1845 – the placing of Labour's sons and
daughters in the possession of *house* and *home*; the making them the
possessors of *their own freeholds*, and the tillers of their own soil, for
their own sole use and advantages. . . . The extreme fineness of the
weather – the sun shining resplendently; the great influx of visitors;
their countenances beaming with joy; the gay holiday dresses; the
galaxy of female beauty present, together with the sight of the

homesteads and bounteous crops, tended to make all feel that
45 O'Connorville was one of the loveliest spots in all creation. . . .
Several small parties were seen in all directions closely scanning the
elegant Chartist villas, the growing crops, the Chartist pigs. . . .

The *Northern Star*, 29 May 1847

Questions

a What was the significance of O'Connor's phrases 'sons of toil'
(line 17), 'my numerous family' (lines 27–8) and 'faithful friend and
bailiff' (line 30)?

b Identify evidence of (i) optimism, and (ii) idealisation in these
two extracts.

c Investigate the background to lines 9–11.

d A cricket match between a side of bricklayers captained by
O'Connor and a side of carpenters was held at the opening of
O'Connorville. On the evidence of these documents, what
aspects of Chartist settlements was such an event meant to
emphasise?

e The *Northern Star* sold an average of 10,000 copies a week
between 1837 and 1852, reaching a maximum of 60,000 in 1839
but slumping to 9,000 by 1843. Why was it popular and what
would account for its decline?

5 The Beginning of the End

Mr. Feargus O'Connor had commenced legal proceedings for the
purpose of recovering rents from the 152 allottees at Snig's End near
Glocester [*sic*]. On Wednesday last bailiffs proceeded from that city
to serve 52 [*sic*] writs. The colonists, who had got intelligence of the
5 coming storm, held a meeting on the preceding evening, and
concerted their arrangements. On the appearance of the bailiffs they
intimated that they would 'manure the land with their blood before
it should be taken from them.' The bailiffs, we understand, did not
make a levy, being convinced by the statements of the colonists that
10 it would be illegal and impracticable, because a most determined
resistance would have been offered to them. The bailiffs, therefore,
retired, and the colonists are now awaiting with some anxiety the
next step of Mr. O'Connor towards his 'children.' – *Cheltenham
Journal*

Quoted in *The Times*, 5 September 1850

Questions

a What was the purpose of serving these writs (line 4)?

b Why did the bailiffs 'not make a levy' (lines 8–9)?

c Comment on the use by the *Cheltenham Journal* of 'colonists' (line 4) and '"children"' (line 13).
d What was the irony about what was taking place at Snig's End? How might this problem have arisen?
e Discuss the viability of the Land Plan.

VIII 1848 – Revival and Decline?

In his autobiography Thomas Cooper wrote of 1848 that 'In the year 1848, I think, Chartists were wilder than we were in 1842, or than the members of the First Convention were in 1838. . . .' and W. E. Adams that 'The history of the Chartist movement is divisible into two periods – the period before and the period after 1848. . . .' In certain senses both were correct in their conclusions. Chartist demands were certainly seen by the authorities as 'wilder' in 1848 than earlier and they were keen to repress the extra-parliamentary activities. It is equally true that after 1848 Chartism lost whatever unity it had, with O'Connor even willing to accede to Household Suffrage while leaders such as Jones and Harney moved towards a socialist perspective to the issue of the working-class vote. This chapter deals with the Chartist agitation in London and in the provinces in 1848 and with the alternative solution offered by Joseph Hume's 'Little Charter'.

The winter of 1847–8 was a severe one. The *Northern Star* talked of the 'extreme prevalence' of influenza, bronchitis, pneumonia, typhus, measles and scarlatina. Smallpox was also widespread. The economy faltered. Henry Reeve ended his diary in 1847 with the following entry

> Remarkable depression in the last months of this year in society; general illness; great mortality; innumerable failures . . . want of money . . . a curious presage of the impending storm. . . .

This was accompanied by increasing Chartist activity. The news of revolution in Paris and elsewhere in Europe which reached England in late February further exacerbated matters. Meetings in London and in the rest of the country proliferated. A Convention was called. There was a further Petition. It was the combination of economic distress and European revolution which convinced the authorities that Chartism really was a threat, for the first time. The situation in Ireland, less than two years after the 'Great Hunger' made matters seem far worse than they in fact were. The twin threats of insurrection in Ireland and a union between Irish nationalists and Chartists in England were conjured up. These circumstances help to explain why the authorities reacted, probably over-reacted, to the resurgent Chartist movement.

Was the Chartist threat real? To the ruling classes it certainly was. Did they not see daily meetings and riots – it was often difficult to distinguish the two – in London? Did they not receive reports of drilling and military style marches from the country? O'Connor was the undisputed leader but when faced by firm action, as on 10 April 1848, he backed away. Other leaders did not have his authority, and anyway they were divided in their counsel. Just as in 1838 and 1839, Chartism was contained from without and critically weakened from within. Yet Kennington Common and Clerkenwell Green are only 'fiascos' in retrospect. Chartism's failure in 1848 and after was not of ideas but of will. The 'moral-force' wing moved away, as indeed it had begun to do in the early 1840s, towards 'respectable' politics: a path which would lead into trade unionism, the emergent Liberal party and eventually Lib-Labism. The physical-force party lost its enthusiasm once good times returned. Others moved in the direction of socialism, an extreme unacceptable to most working people. Chartism may not officially have 'died' until 1860 but after 1848 it never again possessed the dynamism or appeal of the previous decade. And yet Chartist sentiments remained. The Charter, an ultimate dream!

1 1848 – London

(a) Chartism in context

... It was evident, from the new life that seemed to animate the people of almost every European country, that great and stirring events were close at hand. The *Northern Star* of December 4th. (1847), contained accounts of Reform Banquets held at Lille, Avesnes and
5   Valenciennes, in France. About the same time a meeting was held in London to commemorate the Polish Revolution. These events served to rouse the Democracy of England. Ireland was on the *qui vive*. Organization was going on. O'Connor brought the question of the Union between the two countries, before the House of Commons
10 [he had been elected an MP for Nottingham in 1847] and made a motion for a Committee of Enquiry, for which ... he only found twenty-three supporters. A very large public meeting was held in London in favour of justice to England and Ireland, with a view of forming an alliance between the Democrats of both countries. In the
15 Commons, the Government proceeded vigorously with another Coercion Act for Ireland. ... Towards the latter end of December 1847, large gatherings took place in London and many of the provinces. At the former, Julian Harney, Ernest Jones, Carl Schapper

. . . and John Skelton, were the orators. . . . At Dublin, the Con-
20 federalists, or Mitchell party, began to march with great vigour.
James Leach paid a visit to, and addressed this body in January 1848,
and a union of sentiment began to grow up between them and the
Chartists. . . . The news of the French Revolution produced a panic
in the councils of despotism, and filled the Democrats with hope. . . .
R. C. Gammage, op cit, pp 291–2

Questions

a   Why is it important to see Chartism in its European perspective?
b   Why was the Irish dimension an increasingly important element
within Chartism in 1847 and 1848?
*   c   Write short biographies of the leading Chartists mentioned in
this passage.

(b) Trafalgar Square, 6 March 1848

On Monday, March 6th, a public meeting was held in Trafalgar
Square, for the purpose of demanding the repeal of the Income Tax,
or the immediate surrender of the reins of government by the
ministers. It was a middle class meeting, convened by Charles
5   Cochrane. The meeting was, however, proclaimed to be illegal, and
Cochrane cautioned the people against attending; but numbers did
attend, tore the bills to pieces, and elected G. W. M. Reynolds to the
chair. Reynolds had up to this time been widely unknown as a
political speaker, though his fame was widely spread as the writer of
10   several works of fiction. . . . Revolutions and periods of political
excitement push many a man into prominence who might otherwise
have remained in obscurity. The Trafalgar Square meeting was a
golden opportunity for Reynolds. Charles Cochrane had turned
coward and deserted his post; whoever might occupy it in the teeth
15   of the Government proclamation would acquire a reputation for
bravery which another occasion might never afford. . . . Reynolds
occupied the chair without interruption and several speeches were
made against the Income Tax, on the French Revolution, and in
favour of the Charter; and the speaking being at an end, the
20   assembled thousands sent forth vollies of cheers for the People of
Paris and the People's Charter. The meeting dissolved peaceably. A
great crowd followed the chairman up the Strand to his residence in
Wellington-street, where amid loud cheers he addressed them from
the balcony of his house. A portion of the people were, however,
25   more unfortunate. Some well-fed sons of the favoured class, got
remarking on the idleness of the persons attending the meeting. This
levity exasperated the parties attacked, and excitement ran rather
high. This formed a pretext for the police, who attempted violently
to disperse the crowd, and in doing so, exercised no little amount of
30   brutality. The people attempted a defence, and drove the police back

to their quarters; but that force receiving large additions from all quarters, the people were ultimately conquered and many of them taken wounded to the hospital. In the evening, however, a large number again rallied amid cries of 'To the Palace!' and in the
35 direction of Buckingham Palace they proceeded. As in most assemblages of this kind, a number of disorderly persons joined the crowd and broke lamps and windows, and in some instances demanded bread of the bakers and beer of the publicans. They found their way back to Trafalgar Square, and dispersed peaceably. On the
40 two following days crowds collected again and again came into collision with the police, but all ended without anything very serious having occurred.

Ibid, pp 293–5

Questions

a How did the government deal with the meeting and its aftermath?
b In what ways was this a 'middle class meeting' and in what ways was it not?
c What view of violence does Gammage show in this passage?
d Using this passage produce a model for the course of meetings and riots in London in 1848.

(c) The Convention meets 4 April 1848

. . . Almost every European country was now in the throes of revolution; and as each post brought news of the risings and triumphs of the people in Austria, Prussia, the minor German, and many of the Italian states, so appeared to increase the determination
5 of the Chartists and Irish Repealers to establish the long cherished principles for which they had struggled. . . . The long anticipated Convention assembled for business on Tuesday, April 4th, in the John-street Institution, the gallery of which was opened to the public. . . . The delegates then gave their reports. Wilkinson (Exeter) reported
10 that his constituents were opposed to physical force. Matthew Stevenson (Bolton) said there was no use in preaching patience to the starving masses. He described his constituents as being in a most wretched and horrifying condition. Ernest Jones (Halifax) said that his constituents wished to conduct the movement, if possible, on
15 moral force principles, but if necessary, they were ready to fight to a man. . . . James Hitchin described the people of Wigan as suffering from a great amount of oppression and misery. They were ready to try one more Petition, but if it were rejected, they would 'go to work', let the consequence be what it might. . . . O'Connor looked
20 on that Convention as a fair and faithful representation of the people. Chartism was increasing. He believed that he should have five million four hundred thousand signatures on the Petition. The

events in France had given an impetus to the movement. Thrones
were crumbling and tumbling on the Continent; and was it to be
25   expected that England would remain in slavery under such circumstances! On Monday they would go down to the House (meaning
10th. April). . . . He was now becoming a *quasi* minister, and
doubtless would be asked what they intended to do on Monday. On
the faith of that Convention he should reply, that not one pane of
30   glass, nor one pennyworth of property, would be injured. That peace
and good order would prevail, while their grievances were under
discussion. . . . He would be in the procession, in the front row of the
front rank. . . . If the Petition was rejected, he recommended
simultaneous meetings all over the country to address the Queen to
35   dismiss the Ministry, and call to her councils men who would make
the Charter a cabinet question. . . .
        Ibid, pp 299, 301–2, 305

Questions

a   Gammage frequently uses the term 'constituents' in document
     (c) but he did not when writing about the earlier Convention.
     Why?
b   What evidence is there that the Convention was either revolu-
     tionary or conciliatory in tone?
c   O'Connor believed that 'Chartism is increasing'. Discuss
     whether he was correct in his belief.
d   The Convention – a paper tiger?
* e   Assess the tactics which the Chartists employed in the Conven-
        tion. What would you have advocated in early April 1848?

(d) Kennington Common, 10 April 1848

. . . Various bodies continued to arrive on the Common with music
and banners, bearing various inscriptions, such as 'Liberty, Equality,
Fraternity'; 'Ireland for the Irish'. The Convention assembled at nine
o'Clock, Reynolds occupying the chair . . . Doyle also announced
5   that he had received a letter from the Commissioner of Police . . .
[who] stated that the contemplated procession would on no account
be allowed to take place. O'Connor delivered a precautionary
speech; took the blame off the Government for the preparations they
had made, and charged it upon those who had talked of an armed
10   demonstration. . . . The delegates started from the Convention
Room at ten o'clock. The procession was headed by a car, decorated
with various banners and drawn by four horses. This car was to
convey the National Petition. This was followed by a second car,
drawn by six horses, and containing the delegates. On the front seat
15   were Feargus O'Connor, Doyle, McGarth, Jones, Wheeler and
Harney. . . . Having arrived at the National Land Company Offices,
the procession stopped to take up the Petition. . . . The procession at

length reached the Common, where the several bodies of men, with
their bands and banners, formed into a dense mass, estimated at from
20 one hundred and fifty thousand to one hundred and seventy
thousand, and who burst into loud cheering as the delegates' car
came upon the Common.

No sooner had the car reached its destination as O'Connor was
sent for to the Horns' Tavern, where Mr. Mayne, Commissioner of
25 Police, was awaiting him. A report soon spread that O'Connor had
been arrested, but this was an idle rumour. Mayne informed him that
the Government would not interfere with the meeting, but that the
procession would not be allowed. That the Government had the
means of preventing it and that those means would be used and that
30 O'Connor would in that case be held responsible for the consequences. O'Connor promised that the procession should be abandoned. . . . He had led the people to believe that he would head the
procession to the House of Commons and he had pledged himself to
the police that it should be abandoned. . . .

R. C. Gammage, op cit, pp 312–14

(e) I have seen Mr. O'Connor (at about 11-30) & communicated to
him that the petition would not be allowed to pass & every facility
given for that, & its reaching the House of Commons, but no
procession or assemblage of people would be permitted to cross the
5 Bridges.

. Mr O'Connor gave me his word that the procession would not
attempt to cross the Bridges, he added that the Petition should be
sent in Cabs. I had sent Mr Malalieu to ask Mr O'Connor & two or
three of the leaders to come to me to receive such a communication.
10 there was considerable excitement amongst the people as Mr.
O'Connor came to me. it was evidently supposed that he had been
taken into custody. I never saw a man more frightened than he was &
he would I am sure have promised me anything, he had some
difficulty in keeping the people about us on the road quiet, & got on
15 the top of a Cab to tell them he had received a friendly communication on which he was resolved to act.

Memorandum to Sir George Grey, printed in T. A. Critchley,
The Conquest of Violence: Order and Liberty in England, 1970, p
140

(f) 'My children' [O'Connor] commenced, 'you were industriously
told that I would not be amongst you to–day: well, here I am!' and
the crowd burst into a loud cheer. He told them that he had received
one hundred letters urging him not to attend, as his life would be
5 sacrificed; but he replied 'I would rather be stabbed to the heart than
resign my proper place among my children.'. . . 'Yes', he continued,
'you are my children. These are your horses, not mine. I am only
your father and your bailiff, but your honest father and your unpaid

bailiff!' and again was he saluted with a shout of applause. He now
10 commended them not to injure their cause by any act of folly. . . . He
pointed to the Petition, which he said contained the voices of five
millions seven hundred thousands of their countrymen, who would
be looking for good conduct from them that day. . . . He then told
them that the Executive would accompany the Petition, and urged
15 them not to accompany it. . . . The meeting being at an end, the
Petition was placed in three cabs, and the Chartist Executive
accompanied it to the House of Commons. The police guarded the
bridges, and for upwards of an hour after the meeting, prevented any
approach on the part of the people. Some endeavoured to effect a
20 passage, but the police used their staves, often with very little
moderation. The masses, however, did not risk a collision with the
police, and considering the excitement previously existing, the day
passed off in a singularly peaceful manner. On the same day
O'Connor presented the Petition to the House. . . . On the same day
25 [11 April] that the three motions were adopted, an important scene
occurred in the House of Commons on the subject of the National
Petition . . . it was found to contain only one million nine hundred
and seventy-five thousand and ninety-one, and amongst the rest
were signatures such as Victoria Rex, the Duke of Wellington, Sir
30 Robert Peel. . . . There were also a large number of fictitious names,
such as Pugnose, Longnose, Flatnose, Punch, Snooks, Fubbs and
other obscene names. . . . O'Connor afterwards announced that
after what had occurred he should not, for the present, persevere
with the motion of which he had given notice. . . .
R. C. Gammage, op cit, pp 315–19

(g) Reaction

Great preparations were accordingly made. The inhabitants, generally, along the lines of the thoroughfares converging to Kennington
Common, kept close houses – doors and windows shut, and in some
cases, barricaded in stout defence. The measures of the Government,
5 devised and personally worked out by the Duke of Wellington, were
on a large and complete scale, though so arranged as not to obtrude
themselves needlessly on the view. The Thames' bridges were the
main points of concentration; bodies of foot and horse police, and
assistant masses of special constables, being posted at their
10 approaches on either side. In the immediate neighbourhood of each
of them within call, a strong force of military was kept ready for
instant movement . . . At other places, also, bodies of troops were
posted, out of sight, but within sudden command. . . . The public
offices at the West End, at Somerset House and in the City, were
15 profusely furnished with arms; and such places as the Bank of
England were packed with troops and artillery, and strengthened
with sandbag parapets on their walls, and timber barracading of their

windows, each pierced with loopholes for the fire of defensive
musketry.
20   In addition to the regular civil and military force, it is credibly
estimated that at least 120,000 special constables were sworn and
organised throughout the metropolis, for the stationary defence of
their own districts, or as movable bodies to cooperate with the
soldiery and police.

The Annual Register, 1848, Chronicle p 50

(h) Comment

. . . Since the 10th. of April 1848 (one of the most lucky days which
the English workman ever saw), the trade of the mob-orator has
dwindled down to such last shifts as these. . . , But the 10th of April
has been a beneficial crisis, not merely in the temper of the working
5   men, so called, but in the minds of those who are denominated by
them 'the aristocracy'. There is no doubt that the classes possessing
property have faced, since 1848, all social questions with an
average of honesty, earnestness and good feeling which has no
parallel since the days of the Tudors. . . . I have promised to say little
10   about the Tenth of April, for indeed I have no heart to do so. . . . We
had arrayed against us, by our own folly, the very physical force to
which we had appealed. The dread of general plunder and outrage by
the savages of London, the national hatred of that French and Irish
interference of which we had boasted, armed against us thousands of
15   special constables, who had in the abstract little or no objection to
our political opinions. The practical common sense of England,
whatever discontent it might feel with the existing system, refused
to let it be hurled down, on the mere chance of building up on its ruin
something as yet untried and even undefined. Above all, the people
20   would not rise . . . they did not care to show themselves. And the
futility after futility exposed itself. The meeting which was to have
been counted by hundreds of thousands, numbered hardly its tens of
thousands. . . O'Connor's courage failed him after all. He contrived
to be called away, at the critical moment, by some problematical
25   superintendent of police. Poor Cuffy, the honestest, if not the wisest,
speaker there, leapt off the waggon, exclaiming that we were all
'humbugged and betrayed'; and the meeting broke up pitiably,
piecemeal, drenched and cowed, body and soul, by pouring rain all
the way home – for the very heavens mercifully helped to quench
30   our folly – while the monster petition crawled ludicrously away in a
hack cab, to be dragged to the floor of the House of Commons amid
roars of laughter. . . .

Charles Kingsley, *Alton Locke*, 1850 (Everyman edn, 1970), p
16 (Preface 1854) and pp 309–10

Questions

a Using the documents (d) to (h) – it is worthwhile looking again at (c) – produce a narrative of the events of 10 April 1848.

b How did the government over-react to the Chartist threat on 10 April?

c Why was 10 April not a 'fiasco'?

d Why did Charles Kingsley's view of 10 April change between writing *Alton Locke* in 1850 and his preface of 1854?

* *e* The importance of Kennington Common is retrospective rather than contemporary. Discuss.

f O'Connor betrayed the Chartist movement on 10 April 1848. Discuss this indictment of O'Connor.

(i) After the 10th

. . . as early as 6 o'clock, though it rained heavily at the time, groups of people were assembled at the street corners leading into the (Clerkenwell) Green, watching for the arrival of Williams, Fussell, Daly, Sharpe, and the other would-be heroes who had threatened, *vi*
5 *et armis*, to overthrow the Government and sack the Home Office. As the time wore on, the rain ceased, and the numbers assembled on the Green increased considerably. The low population of the neigh-bourhood, attracted to the spot partly by curiosity and partly to have the excitement of a row with the police, loitered along the pavement,
10 and blocked up the entrance to the Green. . . . Not the slightest trace of arms, or of the tendency to employ physical force was visible, and the assemblage presented the usual unmeaning features of a common crowd. . . . Things were in this state until about half-past seven . . . a troop of 60 Life Guardsmen rode at a slow pace through the crowd,
15 which cheered them vociferously as they passed. This sudden apparition had a visible effect upon the assemblage, which began perceptibly to diminish . . . many remained in the hope that Williams and his friends would appear and that the meeting and procession would take place as promised. . . . Whether the formidable look of
20 the Guardsmen, on their black chargers, and the glitter of their cuirasses, had struck terror into Williams and his coadjutors, it is impossible to say, but the position which they ought to have filled was supplied by a poet. . . . On the poet's departure, confusion and uproar began to manifest themselves. Sections of the crowd began to
25 make those desperate rushes, now in one direction and now in another, which generally precede a riot. It was at this critical moment that a strong force of police appeared on the ground. Entering the Green from the east they formed a line across the open space where the people were gathered and swept them at once, with no
30 opposition, into the narrow streets and alleys which open from Clerkenwell-Green on the west. The movement was executed with military precision, and more than 2,000 men who had a moment

before been assembled on the spot disappeared with a rapidity which was almost miraculous. . . .

The Times, 1 June 1848, reporting on a meeting the previous day

(j) . . . the police were nearly run off their legs to keep order . . . where, in these days, many arrests would be made, we, in the 'forties, used to brush the mobs off the streets, and out of the way. The chief thing was to get rid of them. . . . The weapons that were mostly used
5   in the beginning were bludgeons and stones and bricks. There was plenty of ammunition about, because the streets were not what they are now. . . . As for the Chartists' bludgeons, they got them easily enough from trees and fences. . . and in Clerkenwell the police were always coming into conflict with the mob. At first it was a general
10   sort of skirmishing. Men would assemble to go for us and we went for them. . . . A famous battle ground was Clerkenwell Green, and another place I remember well was Cowcross Street. There was plenty of open space on the Green for fighting, and many houses in which the Chartists would hide and throw things at us. . . . Day after
15   day we came into collision with them.

From James Cornish, 'No. LXIII of Survivors' Tales of Great Events: London under Arms. From the Narrative of James Cornish. As Told to Walter Wood', *Royal Magazine*, XXIII, no. 138 (April 1910), p 553

(k) At eleven o'clock Nova Scotia Gardens contained about 900 or 1000 persons of the lowest and most abandoned class, who had met to listen to a speech by a well-known inciter of the people. The first attempt to disperse this dangerous mob proved only partially
5   successful; the mounted police arrived; a cowardly attack was instantly made upon them and the constables by a shower of stones; and after a severe conflict some of the aggressors were captured. On attempting to repulse a mob in a street in Gibraltar-walk, the scene became of a most alarming nature. Every tenement furnished a
10   number of persons who threw missiles at the officers, and yelled and hooted at them in terms of the most appalling execration. The Queen, her progeny, the present Government, with that of the late Premier's, the constitution of the country, the representatives of Parliament, and the Lords Spiritual and Temporal were denounced
15   as accursed, and loud complaints were made of the necessity for a complete social revolution by an equal distribution of the wealth of the country. A feeling of insatiable revenge was repeatedly uttered against the Special constables, as standing in the way of the growing desire for a revolution in England. . . . I heard large numbers of the
20   misguided mob express a determination to conquer the police force at a forthcoming suitable occasion. . . .

Report of Alfred Andrews, a Special constable and artisan

from Hackney on the Bethnal Green riots 4 June 1848; printed in D. Goodway, *London Chartism 1838–1848* (CUP, 1982), p 120

Questions

a   On 2 June 1848 *The Times* concluded that: 'Chartism is neither dead nor sleeping. The snake was scotched not killed on the 10th of April. The advancing spring has brought with it warmth, vigour and renovation'. Given that Chartist meetings continued into August in London, assess the validity of this claim.

b   Were the riots discussed in documents (i) to (k) really about Chartism?

c   What methods did the authorities use to contain the riots? Assess their success.

*   d   The threat of revolution in England in 1848 was never more than an illusion, but to contemporaries a very real illusion. Discuss.

2   1848 – Outside London

(a) In the provinces, things began to look very threatening. In Glasgow the most dire distress prevailed. On the 6th. of March a serious riot took place. The unemployed operatives had expected a distribution of provisions, which, however, did not take place. In a
5   starving condition, and writhing under their cruel disappointment, they proceeded up Irongate and other principal streets, breaking into the provision and gun shops. . . . The excitement became so great that the authorities sent to Edinburgh for more troops. On the following day crowds again collected at Bridgeton where the out
10   pensioners had gathered under arms. A boy threw a clod at one of these and was arrested. A rescue was effected, when Captain Smart, Superintendent of Police, gave the order to fire. The result of this precipitate order was that five persons were shot, and some of them died upon the spot. . . . At Manchester, the people met in front of the
15   Union Workhouse, Tile-street, and demanded the release of the inmates. . . . Manchester, Bradford, Ipswich, Bath, South Shields, Stockport, Sheffield and other places, were marked during the week by large gatherings of people. . . . At Bradford (in May) a tremendous gathering took place. The Executive had despatched M'Douall
20   to that town, in consequence of a rumour of an intended outbreak. Thousands attended from Halifax, Keighley, Bingley and other places. Numbers brandished their pikes in the Halifax procession. The various bodies marched in military order, and paraded the streets of Bradford. They were addressed by Messrs. Lightowler,
25   Shaw, White, Smith and M'Douall. The latter pledged the immense mass to keep the peace – to respect life and property – to arm, but to discountenance any premature outbreak. Not the slightest interfer-

ence took place by the authorities. Bradford was that day in the possession of the Chartists. . . . Intense excitement reigned in
30 Ireland, the manufacture of pikes going on briskly. Physical force still appeared to be organizing too in England. At a Chartist delegate meeting for Lancashire and Yorkshire, held on the 28th. May, a resolution was passed in favour of the formation of a National Guard. . . .

R. C. Gammage, op cit, pp 295, 297

(b) . . . In this year flour was very dear, reaching the price of 5s. per stone, whilst trade was also very bad. This was the time to make politicians, as the easiest way to get to an Englishman's brains is through his stomach. It was said by its enemies that Chartism was
5 dead and buried and would never rise again, but they were doomed to disappointment. It was true that there had been no meetings or processions, nor had the agitation reached the height it attained in 1839, but it was going on. Amongst combers, handloom weavers and others politics was the chief topic. . . . We were only waiting for
10 the time to come again. In 1848 it was said that the year was the year of agitations of revolutions, and thousands of men fell on the field of battle fighting for the people's cause in Europe in this struggle. The French revolution of the 24th. February gave the first impulse to this movement. . . . A great many people in these districts were arming
15 themselves with guns and pikes, and drilling on the moors. Bill Cockcroft, one of the leaders of the physical force party in Halifax, wished me to join the movement, I consented and purchased a gun, although I knew it to be a serious thing for a chartist to have a gun or pike in his possession. I had several years practice in shooting, as the
20 farmer for whom I worked supplied me with gun, powder and shot for the purpose of shooting birds in summer. I saw Cockroft who gave me instructions how to proceed until wanted, which did not occur as the scheme was abandoned. . . . I have been a woollen weaver, a comber, a navvy on the railway, and a barer in the delph
25 [quarryman] that I claim to know some little of the state of the working classes. I well remember only a few years ago talking to a friend who told me he was moulding bullets in the cellar in 1848: he had a wife and five children dependent upon him, but was unable to get work, trade being so bad. Since then, however, under the
30 blessings of free trade and by dint of perseverance he has succeeded in saving a considerable sum and is now living retired from business.

Benjamin Wilson, 'The Struggles of an Old Chartist' in D. Vincent (ed), op cit, pp 206, 209–10

(c) The Government are now getting seriously uneasy about the Chartist manifestations in various parts of the country, especially in London, and at the repeated assemblings and marchings of great bodies of men. Le Marchant told me that . . . lately, accounts have

5   been received from well-informed persons, whose occupations lead
them to mix with the people, clergymen – particularly Roman
Catholic – and medical men, who report that they find a great change
for the worse amongst them, an increasing spirit of discontent and
disaffection, and that many who on the 10th of April went out as
10   special constables declare that they would not do so again if another
manifestation required it. The speeches which are made at the
different meetings are remarkable for their coarse language and
savage spirit they display. It is quite new to hear Englishmen coolly
recommend assassination, and the other day a police superintendent
15   was wounded in the leg with some sharp instrument. These are new
and very bad symptoms, and it is impossible not to feel alarm when
we consider the vast amount of the population as compared to the
repressive power we possess. The extent and reality of the distress
they suffer, the impossibility of expecting such masses of people to
20   be eternally patient and forbearing, to restrain from all their natural
impulses, and endure tamely severe privations when they are
encouraged and stimulated to do otherwise, and are thus accessible
to every sort of internal and external temptation – all these
considerations may well beget a serious presentiment of danger.

> Entry for 3 June 1848, C. C. F. Greville, *A Journal of the Reign
> of Queen Victoria from 1837 to 1852*, vol III, pp 188–90

Questions

a   How far was the Chartism of 1848 in the provinces the result of
    distress and how much of revolutionary zeal?
b   What do these three documents identify as the main cause of the
    revival of Chartism in 1848?
c   In what ways did Charles Greville think that concessions were
    necessary to the working class?
d   Was the Chartism of 1848 different from that of 1839?
e   Why were the provinces more radical than London in 1848?
f   Chartism in 1848 was economic not political in character.
    Discuss.

1848 – compromise and catastrophe

(a) . . . It is evident that the spirit of unity was wanting in the
Chartist body. O'Connor's policy, on the 10th. of April 1848, had
been the main cause of the disunion. . . . O'Connor was wrong, not
in abandoning the procession, but in having encouraged so long the
5   empty braggarts, and enthusiastic but mistaken men of the Convention, and in inducing them, almost to the last moment, to believe that
he would head the procession to the House of Commons. The
boasting which took place on this subject, and the miserable result,
inflicted a wound on Chartism from which it has never recovered.
10   After the 10th. of April, and the exposure of the National Petition,

the Assembly should never have met. It was powerless for good, and made itself simply ridiculous by wasting most of its time in mere talk. . . . Hume's new movement began to agitate out of doors. In some places it was met with approval; but at several meetings the
15 Chartists attended and moved and carried amendments for the Charter. O'Connor denounced the 'four-legged animal', as he called Hume's measure, through the columns of the *Star.* . . . The party of Mr Hume now came more publicly before the people; and at a public meeting held at the London Tavern, on the 16th May 1849, to
20 inaugurate the movement, which meeting was densely attended . . . but the very paper which contained a report of this meeting, contained also a letter from Feargus O'Connor, warning the 'Old Guards' against the new movement. The Chartists continued to hold frequent meetings. . . . One crowded meeting was held in Milton-
25 street Theatre, on June 4th, and was addressed by Reynolds and O'Connor. At this meeting a resolution was proposed by Clark, and seconded by O'Connor, and carried, inviting the Hume-party to a consideration of the Charter. The same week Hume renewed his motion, which met only with eighty-one supporters in the House of
30 Commons. . . . On July 3rd 1849 O'Connor's long-delayed motion for the Charter was brought forward in the Commons, and after a debate, just fifteen, including tellers, voted in its favour. . . . O'Connor now drew towards the Hume-school of Reformers. He attended a meeting at the Standard Theatre and held out the olive
35 branch, telling the meeting that the only object the Chartists had, was to make the rich richer and the poor rich. . . . O'Connor again figured side by side with the Hume-party . . . O'Connor, who had kicked overboard so many men, not for dereliction of principle but on points of policy, who would not have even the name of the
40 Charter altered, who had collected thousands to defeat schemes for Household Suffrage, now gave in his adhesion to a Household Suffrage Association. . . .
R. C. Gammage, op cit, pp 331–2, 347–9

(b) Mr Hume rose to bring forward the motion of which he had given notice, namely –

'That this House, as at present constituted, does not fairly represent the population, the property or the industry of the
5 Country, whence has arisen great and increasing discontent in the minds of a large portion of the People; and it is therefore expedient, with a view to amend the National Representation, that the Elective Franchise shall be so extended as to include all Householders – that votes shall be taken by Ballot – that the duration of Parliaments shall
10 not exceed three years – and that the apportionment of Members to Population shall be made more equal.'
Hume's 'Little Charter' from Hansard's *Parliamentary Debates,* 20 June 1848, col 879; printed with contributions to

the debate by Russell and Cobden in P. Hollis (ed) op cit, pp
352–5

Questions

a   Gammage is very critical of O'Connor's role in the decline of
Chartism in 1848. Is he right?

b   In what ways was the 'Little Charter' different from the 'People's
Charter'? What made the former more acceptable to society as a
whole?

c   Why do you think O'Connor changed his mind on Household
Suffrage?

*   d   If, as O'Connor stated, 'the only object the Chartists had, was to
make the rich richer and the poor rich' why was parliamentary
reform necessary?

Further work

a   The importance of 1848 in the decline of Chartism is something
which historians can identify in retrospect. It was not apparent to
contemporaries. Discuss.

b   In what ways did Chartism develop in the 1850s?

c   What part did Chartists play in the emergence of the Liberal party
in the 1850s and 1860s?

d   Lib-Labism was the natural consequence of working–class
unwillingness to rebel. It was 'respectability' not revolution
which was consciously sought by the vast majority. Discuss.

e   Did Chartism fail?